Torture

Torture

Donatella Di Cesare

Translated by David Broder

polity

First published in Italian as *Tortura* © Bollati Boringhieri editore, Turin, 2016

This English edition © Polity Press, 2018

Polity Press
65 Bridge Street
Cambridge CB2 1UR, UK

Polity Press
101 Station Landing
Suite 300
Medford, MA 02155, USA

ISBN-13: 978-1-5095-2436-5
ISBN-13: 978-1-5095-2437-2 (pb)

A catalogue record for this book is available from the British Library.

Library of Congress Cataloging-in-Publication Data

Names: Di Cesare, Donatella, author.
Title: Torture / Donatella Di Cesare.
Other titles: Tortura. English
Description: Cambridge, UK ; Medford, MA : Polity Press, [2018] |
    Includes bibliographical references and index.
Identifiers: LCCN 2018011377 (print) | LCCN 2018022722 (ebook) |
    ISBN 9781509524402 (Epub) | ISBN 9781509524365 (hardback) |
    ISBN 9781509524372 (pbk.)
Subjects: LCSH: Torture.
Classification: LCC HV8593 (ebook) | LCC HV8593 .D5313 2018
    (print) | DDC 364.6/75–dc23
LC record available at https://lccn.loc.gov/2018011377

Typeset in 10.5 on 12 pt Sabon
by Toppan Best-set Premedia Limited
Printed and bound in Great Britain by Clays Ltd, Popson Street, Bungay,
Elcograf S.p.A.

For further information on Polity, visit our website: politybooks.com

Contents

Prologue

There is something problematic, or at least rather delicate, about the decision to write about torture. Up until just a few years ago, it seemed that it was universally condemned, or at least that it was formally condemned. But that was not enough to stop torture from getting around this prohibition, evading a ban which is so widespread that it has almost risen to the level of a categorical principle. Clandestine, torture seeks refuge behind the scenes.

But this universal stance has weakened. The new adepts of torture are coming into the open practically everywhere. In the United States, they have begun debating it. Shouldn't exceptions be made? Perhaps the considered, limited or even legalized use of torture could again be of service today? It would seem that the 'war on terror' demands as much.

Increasingly, widespread efforts are being made to legitimize a practice that has, in fact, never gone away. Its inveterate champions – the dictators and autocrats, the despots and demagogues who have remained in power across all four corners of the globe – welcome the unexpected breach in democratic ranks, rejoicing at the unexpected opening. Public opinion is swaying, uncertain. It seems that an instinctive rejection of torture is no longer enough.

The prohibition of torture is accused of an empty utopianism, unable to respond appropriately to a global situation dominated by the terrorist threat. This argument holds that we have to protect democracy, and authorizing torture is the way to do it. Only by drawing on terror can we combat terror. For this reason, the question of torture is the watershed that divides two alternative readings of present-day history.

If in this work I am willing to discuss the role and status of torture, the suppositions it rests on and the outcomes it produces, that does not mean that I am prepared to accept some 'good argument' coming along to justify it. A firm 'no' to torture must come before any other discussion can be had. Wherever we start to invoke 'special cases', and wherever a moral philosopher begins a hoary list of exceptions and restrictions, the only appropriate response can be a categorical, concise objection that comes from political practice: 'Do not torture.'

Yet a 'no' driven above all by indignation is not enough to defend the human dignity that torture does so much to wound. This is a theme where we cannot proceed without reflection. In this sense, torture is a paradigm of the moral question in the contemporary age. Theodor W. Adorno cogently summed up the paradox of this problem: 'No man should be tortured; there should be no concentration camps – while all of this continues in Asia and Africa and is repressed merely because, as ever, the humanity of civilization is inhumane toward the people it shamelessly brands as uncivilized' (2004: 285). So, first, there is an impulse to proclaim a decisive and defiant 'no' whenever we find out that someone has been tortured. This is a sense of solidarity with tormented bodies, and it expresses the raw, physical fear of those who identify with the victim. At the same time, there is an attempt to reflect on torture in theoretical terms, indeed in a way that does not just stop at rationalizing this impulse and translating it into abstract principles.

Here, there emerges a contradiction that cuts across the present scenario and which sheds at least some light on the effective impotence that each of us feels today. This is the contradiction between our spontaneous resistance to still having to confront such an intolerable horror and our intellectual understanding of why this horror persists, despite everything, with no end in sight. Torture itself sheds light on the dilemma of the individual who thrashes around, trapped in this vice.

Confronted with such a dramatic scenario, we frankly have
to recognize that 'nothing has changed'. This is, indeed, what
the refrain of Wisława Szymborska's poem 'Torture' tells
us. This work is itself almost a short philosophical treatise.
Even as it offers sharp insight, it also displays an incredulous
bewilderment, an exasperated dismay (2002: 46–7). Perhaps,
faced with repeated horrors, the dogged 'no' of objection
will prove powerless. But it should be remembered that we
are not just what we do, but also what we promise to do,
or not to do.

> Nothing has changed.
> The body is painful,
> it must eat, breathe air, and sleep,
> it has thin skin, with blood right beneath,
> it has a goodly supply of teeth and nails,
> its bones are brittle, its joints extensible.
> In tortures, all this is taken into account.
>
> Nothing has changed.
> The body trembles as it trembled
> before and after the founding of Rome,
> in the twentieth century before and after Christ.
> Torture is, the way it's always been, only the earth
>   has shrunk,
> and whatever happens feels like it's happening
>   next door.
>
> Nothing has changed.
> Only there are more people,
> and next to old transgressions, new ones have
>   appeared,
> real, alleged, momentary, none,
> but the scream, the body's answer for them
> was, is, and always will be the scream of innocence
> in accord with the age-old scale and register.
>
> Nothing has changed.
> Except maybe the manners, ceremonies, dances.
> Yet the gesture of arms shielding the head
> has remained the same.

The body writhes, struggles and tries to break free.
Bowled over, it falls, draws in its knees,
bruises, swells, drools and bleeds.

Nothing has changed.
Except for the courses of rivers,
the contours of forests, seashores, deserts and
   icebergs.
Among these landscapes the poor soul winds,
vanishes, returns, approaches, recedes.
A stranger to itself, evasive,
at one moment sure, the next unsure of its own
   existence,
while the body is and is and is
and has no place to go.

1

The Politics of Torture

The object of persecution is persecution
The object of torture is torture
The object of power is power

George Orwell (1949)

1 Without end? Torture in the twenty-first century

The word 'torture' evokes remote, archaic scenes from the depths of humanity's dark and cruel past. It seems that we need to make this extreme phenomenon a matter of historical reconstruction, as if that could cast it into the distant past for good. The histories of torture – including even the most successful ones – are a repertoire of brutality, a catalogue of horrors, an inventory of atrocities, drawn up against a backdrop of a skeletal, repetitive pattern. Between sadism and perversion, this kind of folklore of evil describes the procedures and techniques that human fantasies devised in order to inflict pain and torment. It lingers over the defencelessness of the victim and the oppressive mask of the torturer; it penetrates into the dark mysteries of the cell where the confession is extracted, infiltrates the chamber of agonies and illustrates the grim feast of punishment. The pillory or the breaking

wheel, the scold's bridle or the whip, the gibbet or the stake
– the scenography of torture is set on the stage of the Inquisition, perhaps because it is there that we identify the peak of
its history. Yet the curtain sometimes falls away, even to the
point that horror and repugnance give way to a feeling of the
sublime that overcomes those who are able to contemplate
the destruction of other people's bodies at sufficient remove.

This story ought to have a happy ending. Progress gets the
better of barbarism and torture is pushed back into civilization's pre-modern past. Cesare Beccaria is a reassuring figure
in this regard. His 1764 treatise *Dei delitti e delle pene* ('On
Crimes and Punishments') strongly condemned torture both
in theory and in practice. He was echoed by Pietro Verri and
the great reformers of the eighteenth century. In this period,
torture was abolished almost everywhere in Europe – in 1740
in Prussia, in 1770 in Saxony, in 1780 in France, in 1786 in
the Grand Duchy of Tuscany and in 1789 in the kingdom of
Sicily. Yet during the modernity of the Enlightenment, torture
remained a troubling presence whose sinister shadow still
hung over civilization. Scenes of torture are repeated over and
over in different and changing forms. Torture resists being
reduced to a phantasmagoria. Monstrous and yet still real, it
forbids any happy ending.

This chapter on the abolition of torture cannot be the last.
Dispensations, exceptions and anomalies have followed one
after another; and this has demanded adjuncts and footnotes.
It seems that torture only ever goes away for a few decades.
It soon reappears on the margins: in conflicts and in wars, at
the boundaries of the modern empires, in the colonies. It
returned with all its ferocious power in prisons under dictatorships and in camps under totalitarian regimes. Even in the
second half of the twentieth century, its advance was unstoppable. How can we forget the atrocities committed in Algeria
and Iran, in the colonels' Greece, in Salazar's Portugal? And
that is not to mention the mass use of torture in the dictatorships of Latin America. This succession of footnotes can only
undermine the narrative of progress. Torture is not a relic of
the Inquisition: it cannot be confined to the peripheries of
time and space. It storms in, unstoppable, from the past. And
it threatens to have a future, too. In the expanded edition of
his now-classic book *Torture*, Edward Peters asked if it was

'without end' (1996: 176). His question picked up on that posed by Piero Fiorelli, the greatest historian of torture, in his monumental work *La tortura giudiziaria nel diritto comune* ('Judicial Torture in Common Law'), published in 1953–4. At the end of that work, Fiorelli inserted a concluding section entitled 'Without an end?' The question is an admission. Torture overwhelms and supersedes history.

Whether it is overt or hidden, combated or tolerated, torture has never been eclipsed. Despite its variations over the centuries, we could even say that it is an uninterrupted phenomenon, a permanent institution and a constant of human history. Laws and legal codes attest to this fact, and so too does the collective memory. It is senseless to claim that torture is a mere aberration reducible to some primitive law, the anomaly of a still-stuttering justice, an accident that happened along the way of reason's march to ultimate victory. We can try to project torture as an obscene brutality of the past in order to convince ourselves that we are living in a paradise in-becoming. Torture corresponds to a distant era, a remote place, a discredited ideology: such are the alibis of a reassuring vision that no longer holds good.

Torture has ducked anathemas and censure, and bypassed bans and prohibitions. It has not been suppressed, nor even left behind. Torture has obstinately hung on, including through the passage from torment to punishment. The new, more sober economy of 'punishment' has not sufficed to get rid of torture. Prison does not expel or banish it from existence. In his famous 1975 essay *Discipline and Punish*, Michel Foucault reconstructs the genealogy of prisons. In what is, in certain regards, a rather optimistic reading, he outlines how torture has become obsolete as a means of punishment. But he also admits that it continues to obsess the penal system. For even as punishment turns from the body to the soul, torture itself adapts. It becomes more subtle and ethereal, but no less fearsome.

Paradoxically, the condemnation of torture encourages its spread by more clandestine means, even in democratic countries. To get a measure of the current extent of the problem, we need only take a look at the data supplied by Amnesty International – according to which, in 2016, at least 122 countries tortured people – and follow the flow of news about

this phenomenon. Such news reaches us not only from theatres of war, refugee camps and the underground lairs of
dictatorships, but also from penitentiaries, jails and all the
internment structures in democratic countries. There thus
emerges an extensive, spectral map of torture. We are forced
to recognize that it has been globalized. The more that torture
is reported and denounced, the more it hides away and cam-
ouflages itself in new forms. As soon as it is abolished, it
re-emerges; after being eradicated, it reappears even more
virulently. And it imposes itself in the actuality of politics, on
the most urgent of agendas.

Even as the ashes of the World Trade Center were smoul-
dering, torture once again became a topic of public debate.
Indeed, faced with the apocalyptic scenario of an imminent
attack in which terrorists were prepared to use weapons of
mass destruction, why should we not resort to torture when
this could secure crucial information and save multiple human
lives? In the 'war on terror', tolerance of torture is the most
striking proof of the immediate and profound erosion of
human rights.

Torture's arrival in the twenty-first century could hardly
have been more glorious. It appears as intelligence's last resort
in keeping a lid on the intermittent global conflict. Previously,
political power had ostensibly prohibited the use of torture,
while at the same time using, or rather abusing, it against
dissent and subversion. Now it asks that this practice be justified, accepted, legalized. Claiming to act in the name of the
people, it pushes for its full authorization. And here, precisely
when it is passed off as an extraordinary expedient measure
for counter-terrorism, torture reveals what was, on closer
inspection, its darkest and innermost face: terror. Torture is
fundamentally inscribed in the logic of domination, of which
it is the most violent and coercive practice. It belongs to the
politics of intimidation, internally even before externally. In
this sense, it displays the omnipotence of sovereignty.

2   Torture and power

We often imagine hell as an eternal punishment. It, and
nothing else, is an unending damnation, which knows neither

release nor redemption. Here, the death sentence translates into torture. The pain hangs over us endlessly, overbearing, as we remain trapped in the corridor of perpetual dying. Torture offers a perverse and ruthless semblance of eternity. This is why it evokes visions of hell. The punishment is perpetual. Yet torture does not stretch over eternity – rather, it is accomplished repetitively, constantly. One of its characteristic traits is this endlessness.

It is no surprise that the tortured person continually yearns for the end, even if that means the definitive end that comes with death. For under torture he is agonized by the distress of interminably dying. As for the torturer, for him the premature death of the victim would be an irritation. His losing consciousness is a mistake to be avoided. The tortured man has to remain conscious and alive, at least as long as the torture is continued. So while torture does very often end with death, it ought not to be mistaken for an execution. It is not a technique of killing. With the death of the other, every relationship is undone, including, and above all, the power relation. Death would free the victim from the torturer's hands in a wretched and paradoxical release. This is why torture is not fulfilled by the victim's death; rather, this death marks the moment in which a prolonged practice of violence loses its object too soon, even as it triumphs in its atrocity. Its ultimate goal is not elimination. Torture goes further, turning dying into an enduring punishment, transforming a human being into a moribund creature.

We can only grasp the political importance of torture when we consider it as the exercise of an absolute violence. Here, its close link with power becomes apparent. Torture is first of all the power to dominate the other, to overwhelm him with torment, to make him submit through suffering, to subjugate him with mistreatment. It has no limit except death itself – and the victim's death is something to be forestalled.

The pain felt by the tortured man is the mark of the torturer's terrible and untrammelled power. It is a pain that he must feel in the most intimate recesses of his being. The torture scene sets the defenceless victim, disgraced in his humiliation, against a triumphant butcher at the apotheosis of his sovereignty. While the victim is conceded nothing, for the torturer anything is possible. He makes his victim's tortured body a canvas onto which he can transcribe punishment. He works away at the flesh, for this is the site of his experiments, the material for his technique of destruction. The torturer is an artisan playing the Creator, asserting himself as the lord of pain. The other, dehumanized person is reduced to nothing but his own passive corporeality. Even when the torturer strikes the soul, the mental pain is mistaken for physical pain, and vice versa. The victim's suffering body enters into a torture machine that is equipped with ever-new devices and mechanisms, with instrumentation to be put to the test. The torture is not the dock for a trial but the laboratory of a destructive imagination.

Violence brings pain; it lays it bare and makes it visible and audible. Speech is suffocated by the series of wounds, blows and pummellings. There is no place, here, for articulated sounds, only moaning and screaming. Even as the violence seeks to penetrate deep into the victim, into their most intangible inner life, in order to turn it inside out and take hold of it, it undermines this same enterprise by destroying the victim's language. It can tear out his innards while he is still alive, just as ancient torment did. But this leaves the torture victim as a body without a voice.

This contradicts an idea that has long enjoyed a certain consensus, which holds that torture's ultimate purpose is to extract a confession of the truth, as if the punishment were by itself justified, as if the person subject to it were almost to blame. This moral somersault, the foundation on which a centuries-long fiction was built, sought not only to unburden the butcher of his responsibilities but also to pass off torture as an instrument of confession.

Only when torture is freed of its fraudulent links with the Truth, and when the alibi of interrogation collapses, is it revealed for what it is and has always been: the violent practice of power. Torture should be considered not in terms of the codes of truth but in those of the code of power. Perhaps no one has exposed the status of torture as well as Franz Kafka, who pointed to its close connection with the laws of power. His famous short story *In the Penal Colony*, written in 1914 and published in 1919, is a complex and astonishing allegory revolving around a 'peculiar apparatus' (*ein eigentümlicher Apparat*), a singular device. There are multiple resonances here: the apparatus calls to mind the workings of technology, escaping, undermining and supplanting its controller; it represents the war machine that promises salvation yet brings destruction; it points to the alienation of labour, the consumption fetish and the monstrosity of an inhuman progress.

There are many troubling questions in Kafka's sun-drenched colony. This is the site of a traditional extra-territoriality, situated on the border between *Le Jardin des supplices* and *L'Univers concentrationnaire*. It is inhabited by impersonal shadows, the officer, the soldier, the traveller, and the condemned man who exchange masks, roles and fates. Yet the function of the apparatus is clear: it is a sort of printer that kills as it writes. The machine engraves the sentence on the body of the condemned man.

The story begins with the preparations for the execution of a soldier, who has been accused of indiscipline and insulting a superior. But the apparatus is archaic and out of use, and it proceeds according to a slow ritual which lasts at least twelve hours. Only thus can it stamp the vowels and consonants, and indeed the flourishes and arabesques that must sublimate pain and death, even if this means stretching out the punishment. Hence the torture must be brought to its proper conclusion before the execution takes place. The officer, both judge and executioner, invites the traveller to sit 'on the edge of the pit' between life and death. The traveller represents the modern European world, where the death penalty no longer exists – the world where it can be said that 'We had torture only in the Middle Ages'. But from his perch he can witness the brief interregnum of torture, a spectacle from another epoch that most have since deserted.

The apparatus is both a mechanism of justice and a mechanism of death. The officer explains the judicial customs that govern the colony: 'The basic principle I use for my decisions is this: Guilt is always beyond a doubt.' And here 'special measures' are applied. There is no trial – neither a defence, nor an admission of guilt, nor a confession of truth. What would be the use if guilt is always already supposed in advance? The truth, the only truth, is the one contained in the sentence itself. It is not worth making the condemned man aware of the sentence in advance, for 'He experiences it on his own body'. Kafka overturns the logic of justice in order to shed light on torture. And, paradoxically, this allows everything to appear in a clearer light. The tortured man is not called on to speak: a lump of felt is pushed into his mouth to stop him from screaming.

His naked body is inserted into the mechanism that will produce the truth. If he wants to at least understand his punishment, he will have to decipher the sentence as it is inscribed upon his body. His back – as Benjamin observed (1999: 129) – is a writing surface, his skin a blank page. The needles sink into his skin; the blood is washed away with water in order to preserve the beauty of the incision. The apparatus is performative: it turns words into deeds. Such was the wish of the earlier Commandant who designed it. Only the transcription of the punishment allows for guilt to be cancelled. Here, sentencing and punishment is one and the same thing. The law is torture and torture is the law. In the penal colony, that is what legislation is. Torture is the sentence inscribed on the body of the condemned man. In Kafka's officer's words, '"Our sentence does not sound severe. The law which a condemned man has violated is inscribed on his body with the Harrow. This Condemned Man, for example," and the Officer pointed to the man, "will have inscribed on his body, 'Honour your superiors'"' (Kafka 1919).

Kafka did not only turn his searching and implacable gaze on the mechanism of torture. He also identified what most troubled it: *lèse majesté*. Torture is the response to anyone who, even unwittingly, challenges the law of power. Tellingly, in Kafka's story, the soldier is accused of insubordination. This is an exemplary accusation in the sense that it clearly states what crime is implicit whenever anyone is condemned to torture: *crimen majestatis*. This crime is a challenge to the principle of sovereignty and the untrammelled legitimacy of power. Reacting with what is an extreme – and yet ever-available – practice, power seeks to reassert that even the slightest crime is an attack on the law itself. As Foucault puts it, 'in every offence there was a *crimen majestatis* and in the least criminal a potential regicide' (Foucault 2014: 50). Torture is never used for the sake of seeking the truth. Quite the contrary, it is power's own truth that is reinstated through its inscription on the body of the tortured, with the triumph of the sovereign's vengeance.

At the end of the story, the apparatus refuses to write the imperative *Sei gerecht!* ('Be just!'). Running out of control, the blind machine vomits up the gearwheels of its enigmatic mechanism, one after the other. The debris strikes the officer – himself, a cog in the military hierarchy, an emblem of mediocre servitude and obedient discipline. His petrified face shows no sign of redemption. The revolt of the torture machine turns the torturer into the tortured. This is the cipher for a bitter revenge. The explosion enables a terrible payback.

Torture does not re-establish justice, but reactivates power. The torture machine, a branding mechanism, ultimately proves transparent: writing power's truth on the body, it inscribes power into the logic of sovereignty. This reappropriation strategy is always lurking. No political form is left unscathed – not even democracy. The spectacle of torment may cease but that does not mean torture has gone away. Even when the verdict is carved into the soul, the political technology of the body continues to function. After all, the soul is itself a tool of power exercised on the body. Torture remains resolute, indelible, in the darkest site of the political ritual where sovereignty, which has been only momentarily wounded, reconstitutes itself, unlike the tortured person, who continues to be the enemy. The supremacy of power crashes down on her body, and this is not the supremacy of law but that of physical force because, in breaking the law, the transgressor has attacked sovereignty itself.

In the last analysis, a politics of torture is a politics of terror. Once it is unleashed, the presence of sovereign power is printed on the tortured body.

3 The dark backdrop of sacrifice: torture in the mechanisms of terror

Wherever terror breaks out, there also emerges torture. There is a deep complicity between the two; their connivance is intimate and secretive. Torture seemed like an anachronism that had been eclipsed by the modern state, in which terror itself stagnated. It was almost as if terror had serenely dozed off. But that was only briefly the case – and was, in fact, an illusion. Terror and torture have forcefully returned, appearing as the most urgent of problems. Terror calls for torture. It appeals to a sovereignty which extends beyond the law, a terrain in which even torture suddenly becomes legitimate again. Both are political rituals that mark and inscribe power on bodies. They disturb and disconcert. They prove simultaneously to be both pre-modern and post-modern, unacceptable and yet accepted in public space.

The background of political power is the enduring possibility of the recourse to violence – i.e. violence understood as sovereignty and as a monopoly of force. Even when the state never actually has to use its weapons, it protects its citizens' lives by way of the threat of death. Then there are the citizens themselves. Fearing the state's destructive power, they submit to it. The recognition of political power depends on fear and the need for security. If violence is implicit in order, order is implicit in violence. Democracy makes us forget this vicious cycle. Nonetheless, it is no abler to break out of this cycle than any other political form. Even within a framework of legality, the state may rapidly transform into a police state. Liberty gives way to security; the suspect is subjected to preventative arrest, special tribunals are established and torture is reintroduced. All of a sudden, it becomes apparent that political power is based on the possibility of resorting to force. And this is a power that each citizen may feel on their own skin. So what, then, will protect citizens from the arbitrary power of the state?

It would, nonetheless, be mistaken simply to identify terror with violence. There is a more complex relationship between the two, as Hannah Arendt makes clear in her 'Reflections On Violence': 'Nowhere is the self-defeating factor in the victory of violence over power more evident than in the use of terror to maintain domination . . . Terror is not the same as violence; it is, rather, the form of government that comes into being when violence, having destroyed all power, does not abdicate but, on the contrary, remains in full control' (Arendt 2002: 33).

If we are to understand how torture arises – or better, the reasons why it persists into the present – then we need to scrutinize the symbolic matrix of the political violence that produces terror. Yet this is what we are normally so careful to avoid doing. If torture occupies a special place in our shared imaginary, it is because we try to push it back into an almost exotic remoteness, distant from ourselves in both space and time. In so doing, we are attempting to exorcise torture, to deny its troubling proximity. This attempt is surely eased by the fact that the spectacle of torment has faded. In modern times, this spectacle is replaced by torture as a secret practice – a practice which persists, despite everything, side by side with penitentiary reform. Torture continues to be practised behind the scenes, in locations closed off to the public. This is a ritual that is entrusted to agents who operate in the shadows of state power; it is carried out in such a manner that it can be recused, belied, denied. In its modern form, torture takes on the opaque character of deniability. We know about it, but we must not see it happening. Such a political practice cannot take place within the public space, yet it must also weigh on that same space, and indeed loom over it, so that the threat it poses might be effective. This is why when torture breaks out in all its cruelty, it is immediately labelled illegal.

If liberalism is to be believed, torture is but a violation, a dysfunction, a pathology. It is the outcome of a power imbalance. Liberal morality is convinced of the equal dignity of and respect for each individual. Hence this imbalance can only be seen as violating and jeopardizing the foundational contract. Liberalism has nothing further to say about torture except that it is, indeed, prepared to legalize the use of torture, on an exceptional base, in the face of terror.

This ambiguous reticence is rather telling. For torture itself reveals an undeniable convergence between democracy and totalitarianism, just as Giorgio Agamben identified in his *Homo sacer* (2017: 12). Torture flows back through the underground river of biopolitics, pulling along in its current the life of the killable and unsacrificeable *homo sacer*. Though Agamben does not himself mention this, torture is the ritual that has inscribed naked life in the state order from its outset. And precisely on account of this beginning, this *arché*, torture is fearsomely archaic.

Perhaps we can more clearly show the value of torture when we set it within a theological-political context. Looking at the archaeology of torture, we see how this ancient writing engraved sovereign power on the body. This was not just any violence. Rather, it was a form of sacrifice that imprinted this power's sacred presence. Sovereign power's signature was not the contract but the sacrifice. It was the torture victim that allowed the sovereign's mystical body to manifest itself. Sovereign torture immediately contributed to power, to its consolidation and its recognition.

Even in secularized modernity, where political theology remains in the background, sovereignty has not broken its link with sacrifice (cf. Kahn 2008). Instead, the sacrificial violence becomes more diffuse, more common. In its various forms, it becomes an ordinary condition of life.

Even in the realm of popular sovereignty, citizens are called upon to make sacrifices. And power continues to reveal itself in the body. But the sovereign that manifests itself in the sacrificial act is popular sovereignty. For evidence of this, we need only look at the Tomb of the Unknown Soldier – a monument not to the unknown but to all. The citizen is prepared to sacrifice himself as the state requires because he identifies himself with this same sovereignty. This does not mean that he may not sometimes consider this demand for violence unjustified, an abuse of power; the sacrifice is then nothing but a senseless death.

But if the citizen's body is the immediate site of his power, how then is it possible for it to be tortured? It must be that there remains some obscure bedrock of power within the modern state, which eludes the citizen and remains unpenetrated by popular sovereignty. This would be the opaque, hidden, always deniable presence of the mystical body of a sacred sovereignty. And this latter draws on torture. However, this is no longer the ritual of sovereign torture, in which the individual was sacrificed to the power that could thus draw advantage from such a sacrifice. For here there is no longer any reason for triumphalism. Power needs credibility, yet even according to the terror mechanism itself, in this case the citizen has been killed, not sacrificed – and nor could he have been. This is what each person must necessarily be shocked into recognizing when they see the torture perpetrated by the state: that they are suddenly nothing but naked life. Beyond the facade of the citizen, there emerges the *homo sacer*.

So when torture resurfaces in the modern state, it has an archaic patina, a sacral stamp. This offends us and wounds popular sovereignty. But abolition has never been able to get rid of torture.

4   Torture after the abolition of torture

Over the last two centuries, a great abolitionist movement sought to put a final stop to torture. Yet this practice has never gone away. Instead, it has transformed and adapted itself to the new circumstances. As Serge Portelli has observed, torture has 'passed from the procedural code to the penal code' (2011: 12). Abrogated by law, it has become a clandestine practice in the shadows of sovereignty.

While Beccaria's arguments were set down on paper, and still remain valid, the fight against torture has assumed a different character. It is no longer normative but a labour of critique. The question of principle is no longer up for discussion. For a long time – at least, until the twenty-first century – it was unthinkable that anyone could continue to make apologies for torture. The condemnation was too driven, too well-justified, too resolute. It was inserted in the Declaration of the Rights of Man and the Citizen as early as 1789; this document's ninth article affirmed the presumption of innocence and established a prohibition against excessive harshness: 'As all persons are held innocent until they shall have been declared guilty, if arrest shall be deemed indispensable, all harshness not essential to the securing of the prisoner's person shall be severely repressed by law.'

Almost everywhere, once torture was declared illegal it passed from one side of the threshold to the other: it was downgraded from the mother of ordeals to the dark and fearsome accomplice of power. And the state adapted: it 'outlawed' torture but continued to practise it or, better, had it practised illicitly in a more or less hidden fashion. So how can we fight against torture if the criminal is the state itself? Or, indeed, if the state denies it is carrying out such a practice? Or if the state refuses to admit any responsibility, invoking its own legislation which officially forbids this practice? Most importantly, if the the state is itself the transgressor, who will ascertain its guilt? For it is obvious that the criminal will avoid being subjected to any judgement. Indeed, the problem is all the more complex in that the torturer who once operated in broad daylight now hides away, disappearing in the labyrinth of the state apparatus. And the state is inevitably going to defend and shelter him. For the persecutor tacitly allows the repression. The responsibility appears simultaneously both collective and fragmentary. Who should answer for the torture perpetrated by the state?

After the genocides of the twentieth century, which confounded any dream of progress, torture – trustingly considered as the recrudescence of a totalitarian 'barbarism' – faced the stigma of international public opinion. This latter had gained a greater understanding, a greater sensitivity towards the magnitude of the crimes that had been perpetrated. The role that systematic torture had played in the service of extermination in the camps spread disturbance, fear and alarm. Appeals were made to human dignity, and there was a search for the rules that would be able to defend humanity from itself. Torture was made to answer for itself in the courts where these heinous criminals were judged; it became a question of international law. In the immediate post-war period, the UN solemnly prohibited torture. The fifth article of 1948's Universal Declaration of Human Rights states that 'No one shall be subjected to torture or to cruel, inhuman or degrading treatment or punishment.' These words seem to mark a historical watershed, a point of no return. But fundamentally, they are just words. Legally they are a *ius cogens*, an imperative and binding norm. But this norm has no practical effect and proves easy to get around (cf. Harrasser, Macho and Burhardt 2007).

It was Europe, the theatre of the world wars and the fatherland of the Holocaust, which took the next step with a document that outlined a sanction for torture. This call first appeared in the European Convention for the Protection of Human Rights and Fundamental Freedoms. Signed in Rome on 4 November 1950, its third article prohibits torture. Judges took charge of ensuring that this prohibition was respected by all member states. Thus a European Court of Human Rights (ECHR) was established in 1959, headquartered in Strasbourg. Every European citizen can make recourse to the ECHR. The Court is slow to intervene, and it does so only ex post facto; the convictions which it issues are of limited effect. Without doubt, there are also examples of abuses and transgressions. Yet the Court's judgements have acquired authority and influenced public opinion.

Torture continued in Europe – the United Kingdom carried it out in Ireland, and France in Algeria – and across the rest of the world, from Latin America to the communist countries, from Asia to Africa, and in North America. States know this, but they deny it; they do not question the principle but rather keep torture under a veil of secrecy. It is a dirty secret; unlike in the case of the death penalty, here they do not put what they are doing on display.

Then there is the attempt to elaborate legal instruments and create international bodies that can closely monitor torture around the world. The finish line came with the Convention against Torture and Other Cruel, Inhuman or Degrading Treatment or Punishment adopted by the UN's General Assembly on 10 December 1984, entering into effect on 27 June 1987. This convention represents the most important medium of the fight against torture, which its first article defines as follows:

> the term 'torture' means any act by which severe pain or suffering, whether physical or mental, is intentionally inflicted on a person for such purposes as obtaining from him or a third person information or a confession, punishing him for an act he or a third person has committed or is suspected of having committed, or intimidating or coercing him or a third person, or for any reason based on discrimination of any kind, when such pain or suffering is inflicted by or at the instigation of or with the consent or acquiescence of a public official or other person acting in an official capacity. It does not include pain or suffering arising only from, inherent in or incidental to lawful sanctions.

However, the originality of this Convention lay not so much in the way in which it defined torture as in the absolute prohibition that it set out in its second article: 'No exceptional circumstances whatsoever, whether a state of war or a threat of war, internal political instability or any other public emergency, may be invoked as a justification of torture.' Most decisive was the creation of a Committee against Torture, made up of ten experts tasked with monitoring and reporting cases of torture. The limits of this committee's activity became clearer in smaller theatres like the Committee for the Prevention of Torture. This committee was established by the European Convention for the Protection of Human Rights and Fundamental Freedoms in 1987 and was also authorized to make periodic preventative inspections.

International institutions were complemented by effective non-governmental organizations like Amnesty International – keeping up its fight against torture and the death penalty ever since 1961 – and Human Rights Watch, the most important human rights organization in the United States. Faced with the very great number of violations – speaking even of a 'global crisis' – in 2000, Amnesty launched the Stop Torture campaign.[1]

Nonetheless, we cannot fail to highlight a certain paradox here: while there is a proliferation of committees and NGOs, legal instruments, tribunals and criminal courts – the most important being the International Criminal Court established in 1998 – torture does not in fact retreat, still less disappear, under the threat of international law. For in the last analysis, that would mean that states would have to condemn themselves. Yet even those states that ratified the 1984 Convention against Torture (as of 2015, 176 of them have done so), ignore complaints and reprimands, unless they are likely to be truly discredited. So it is precisely the official condemnation of torture that encourages it to spread in clandestine form.

5   The black phoenix

Fighting against torture means seeking its traces in the shadows. It means monitoring state practices and abuses. It means reporting on a power that acts in secret; a power which, at constant risk of illegitimacy, reacts not just with intimidation but with violence. Hence the decisive role played by the media. But knowledge does not always mean the ability to act. And the mountain of information can even

---

[1] https://www.amnesty.org/en/get-involved/stop-torture/

increase the sense of powerlessness in what is often an uneven struggle, in which the criminal is almost always the state. The internet has contributed to monitoring and transparency. We need only think of the secret files of the Guantánamo detainees that were revealed by Wikileaks.[2] But often the power relations remain unchanged. While we know that China tortures lawyers who stand up for human rights – such as Yu Wensheng, who was held in the Daxing detention centre near Beijing from October 2014 to January 2015 – sadly this knowledge does not allow any effective intervention.[3]

The globalization of torture further complicates this picture. Techniques, methods and experience can easily be exported. Even in a historical perspective, we can see an unbroken chain: if France's Sûreté introduced torture with magnets in Indochina, South Vietnam also had internment camps of its own, the most famous of them on the island of Poulo Condor. In these camps, it resorted to extreme practices, ranging from electric shocks to *falaka* – i.e. blows dealt to the soles of the feet. And this is not to mention the expertise that the Nazis brought with them when they left Germany after 1945. One case in point was Klaus Barbie. Having evaded the prosecutors of the Nuremberg Trials, from 1947 on, he made a decisive contribution to the US secret services. Barbie collaborated with the US army's Counter Intelligence Corps in the context of the emerging Cold War. In 1951, he managed to board a ship to Buenos Aires from Genoa, using the false identity 'Klaus Altmann'. He was a teacher in torture first in Argentina and then, from 1955, in Bolivia. He participated in the bloodiest of endeavours.

But not only are the torturers exported. In recent years, there has been an increased 'offshoring' of the detainees themselves, particularly at the hands of George W. Bush's administration. They are handed over to friendly countries that have more familiarity with torture and less monitoring. This is called 'extraordinary rendition'. The prisoners, for the most part terrorism suspects, are taken to secret detention centres. Some of these are even in Europe, for instance

---

[2] https://wikileaks.org/gitmo/
[3] China: Submission to the UN Committee against Torture (ASA 17/2725/2015).

in Poland and Romania. The United States, moreover, has used ships kitted out as prison galleys floating, for example, outside Diego Garcia, a British territory in the Indian Ocean which is also the site of an American military base.[4] Clearly, what it was looking for here was extraterritoriality, just like in Guantánamo.

But even after Obama decided that this internment camp would be closed, this did not mean that extraordinary rendition came to an end. Many former prisoners have been extradited to third countries. In July 2016, Italy decided for humanitarian reasons to take in the Yemeni citizen Fayiz Ahmad Suleiman. He had been detained at Guantánamo for fourteen years.

Here, two closely connected phenomena come to light. Even many states that declare torture illegal do in fact practise it to a more or less concealed degree when they invoke 'emergency' policies, appeal to 'exceptional' circumstances or even proclaim a state of exception. It is for this purpose that they play with the meaning of 'torture', attempting to define it more narrowly. Moreover, as torture spreads, it is gradually dissembled by the use of more refined – but nonetheless violent – methods that manage not to leave a trace. This 'white torture' is designed to be invisible after the fact. Its methods range from forced sleep deprivation to spatial-temporal disorientation, from immobilization to isolation, from sexual violence to psychological torment, and from simulated execution to all manner of physical and emotional humiliation. Thus even after torture was apparently banned, it transformed into something else to the point that it went beyond the classic concept and put the definitions of the past to the test.

Everything conspires to ensure that a veil of silence soon falls and that torture is forgotten. The privilege of immunity is thus offered to those who torture for the state, or worse, do so without its knowledge, be they policemen, secret service agents, paramilitaries or private militias, following the widespread tendency to subcontract the monopoly of violence.

---

[4] The documentation has been published by the NGO Reprieve. See http://www.reprieve.org.uk/press/2014_07_09_diego_garcia_rendition_documents_damage/

Torture is practised behind the scenes in a space that becomes wider and more uncontrollable. The reticence becomes better armoured and the silence more unyielding. Torture is fought against, yet also tolerated. Like a black phoenix, it repeatedly vanishes and then takes form again in a fresh set of circumstances.

6 Torture and democracy

Torture's clandestine spread does not stop at the external borders of democratic countries. In the last decades of the twentieth century, there prevailed the belief that torture was linked to violent political forms – the residue of the variants of so-called 'totalitarianism' – or that it was a savage and ruthless weapon wielded by dictatorial regimes. When totalitarianism faded away, starting with its manifestation behind the Iron Curtain, and when countries such as those in Latin America returned from dictatorship to democracy, torture was supposed to disappear from the face of the planet. In its more or less ingenuous or innocent forms, this conviction reassured us to the point of stopping us seeing what was happening in many western countries, for instance in 1970s Italy and Germany. It was based on the assumption that democracy was the only real deterrent to torture: 'More democracy, less torture!' It acted as if democracy were somehow immune to torture, as if democracy opened up a new world of law, rectitude and morality, and began a new chapter of the history of humanity in which torture could no longer have any share.

In recent years, a taboo has been broken: namely, the taboo which saw the democratic ethos as the failsafe against all abuse and violence. There was a real paradigm shift in the wake of 9/11 as the biggest western democracy declared a state of exception. In so doing, it recognized the use of torture, and provided part-justification for it as a means of combating terrorism. The United States has therefore jeopardized the few conquests that have been made in the domain of human rights, creating a precedent of still unmeasurable proportions. For if the United States uses coercive methods from time to time, why shouldn't the Asian and African states, who have always been subject to such scrutiny, do so? Why wouldn't the Russians be justified in doing so in Chechnya, or the Indians in Kashmir?

The violation of the taboo, with the decline of the immediate tie binding torture to totalitarian and dictatorial regimes, has however had one advantage. Namely, it has exposed a phenomenon that had long been taking shape, and to which we had preferred to turn a blind eye: the effective democratization of torture. In his 2007 book *Torture and Democracy*, a monumental *summa* of current forms and methods of torture, the Iranian-American political scientist Darius Rejali highlighted the hypocrisy of the democracies that employ ever more sophisticated means of torture precisely in order to avoid leaving traces, and thus save face. As Rejali observes (2007: 21), this is no longer a matter of asking ourselves if and why torture might be compatible with democracy, but rather 'how' it is compatible.

Even democracies can live with torture. And indeed, they do live with it – they accept it within their own countries, in more or less latent or explicit ways, depending on the circumstances and the sensibility of public opinion. But modern states can also torture, if necessary, without worrying too much about the spread of disapproval among their citizens. The surveys show us how malleable public opinion is, even in western countries. In an article published in April 2009, Mark Danner writes that, 'Polls tend to show that a majority of Americans are willing to support torture only when they are assured that it will "thwart a terrorist attack"' (Danner 2009). Commenting on the latest figures in a 2011 essay, Rejali emphasizes that the 'majority favoring torture is a very recent, post-Obama phenomenon' (2011: 40).

Democracy does not prevent or impede torture. The reason for this is quite simply that torture does not depend on any specific political form. It is flexible enough to be able to survive, amidst a wider democratic context. Or, rather, we could say that the democratization of torture, its persistence, reveals the hidden void at the very centre of democracy, as this latter is split between constitutional sovereignty and mental power (see Agamben 2005: p. 3 ff.; 2009). In other words, torture itself reveals that the mystery of politics is not a matter of laws but rather of policing.

7   After 9/11: state of exception, pre-emptive torture

On the morning of 11 September 2001, four passenger jets were hijacked by 19 members of al-Qaeda. They were smashed into carefully chosen targets, each of them symbols of US power: the Twin Towers in New York and a wing of the Pentagon in Washington. The attacks dramatically marked the beginning of the new millennium. The world had entered a new era. The United States reacted by declaring the 'war on terror'. This expression, first used by President George W. Bush on 20 September 2001 in a joint session of the US Congress, was adopted and repeated across the whole West. The 'war on terror' was directed against organizations classified as 'terrorist', as well as all the so-called 'failed states' – no longer recognized as states – and 'rogue states'. A few days later, on 7 October, Operation Enduring Freedom brought the invasion of Afghanistan and the subsequent overthrow of the Taliban regime. Not long after that, on 19 March 2003, the attack was launched against Saddam Hussein's Iraq. The latter was accused of supporting al-Qaeda and possessing weapons of mass destruction, accusations that both proved to be unfounded.

The expression 'war on terror' – just like 'battle against evil' – is a metaphor well suited to making the 'war' unlimited in both space and time. A 'war on terror' could be never-ending, all the more so given that the enemy is not easily identifiable, and is instead only defined on the basis of its actions. The 'war on terror' offered the US administration not only the advantages of an unlimited war but also the pretext to suspend civil liberties, strengthen executive power and declare a state of emergency through the Patriot Act, which was passed by a near-unanimous Congress vote on 26 October 2001. In a scenario increasingly taking the shape of a Manichean conflict – not least thanks to the narrative provided by the major TV networks – the world's leading democracy abandoned multiple democratic prerogatives. Aimed at preventing terrorist attacks, among other things the Patriot Act handed extraordinary powers to police and intelligence agencies, expanded surveillance over communications and stepped up immigration controls through the use of digital fingerprinting. Thanks to a decree signed by Bush on 13 November 2001, 'terrorist suspects' could be expelled, or held indefinitely, and judged by extraordinary military tribunals behind closed doors and without a presumption of innocence. The emergency was then normalized. What had been extraordinary became ordinary, and the suspension of the law was pursued indefinitely. This left a deep scar on America's image of itself and the world's image of America. An ancient philosophical question was thus once again posed: what use is there in trying to defeat evil if it is necessary to become evil in order to do so? Or in its new version: what use is there in defeating the anti-democratic forces of terror if in the process it is necessary to use terror and betray democracy? About three thousand people had been killed in the 9/11 attacks. Four years of 'pre-emptive war' in Iraq caused the deaths of large numbers of Iraqis, 60,000 according to the Iraq Body Count, and 600,000 according to the *Lancet* medical journal. There is no great difficulty in comparing these figures: between 20 and 200 Iraqis were killed for every victim of 9/11. The escalation that came with the 'war on terror' brought devastation, slaughter and brutality which are still difficult to get the measure of today. The 'western values' exported in this manner have been compromised – perhaps forever.

Terrorizing the terrorists – such was the chosen strategy in a spiral of violence that obeyed the requirements of seeking symbolic 'compensation'. But terrorizing the terrorists also means becoming the mirror image of the terrorists, indeed their even more determined and resolute reflection, almost as if to prove that democratic values do not weaken the capacity for retributive action. In the 'battle against evil', everything is permitted, even the recourse to illegal measures. It does not matter that terrorism has not been defeated, that the violence has not been reduced and that on the contrary it has boosted the recruitment of fresh waves of jihadists.

In punishing the 'evil angels', perhaps nothing could appear a more effective weapon than torture – a form of retributive terror. Nothing has demonstrated better than torture the moral collapse of the United States. Torture had continued to be refined in semi-clandestine conditions. Now it came to the surface, as the US administration declared it a necessity. Torture was welcomed into public debate, and for the first time in a democracy it was officially acknowledged that it was taking place. This was the novelty after 9/11: it no longer seemed obvious that torture should be condemned.

This is a war whose fronts are not well defined, in which the enemy hides away by acting intermittently, with *coups de main*, and with sudden and lightning-quick operations. In such a context, the conflict is decided by information and news that is gathered behind the scenes, in the zone of shadows in which torture prospers. We need only think of partisan warfare, guerrilla warfare and wars of liberation like in Algeria. This is not to say that interrogating the enemy was not also a decisive strategic weapon in traditional warfare. Yet the Geneva Conventions of 1949, which protected the rights of 'enemy' prisoners of war, have established a strong deterrent against the use of torture.

The 'war on terror' has, however, allowed the United States – itself a signatory of these conventions – to get around this obstacle by inventing a new, extraordinary category of 'enemy': namely, the 'unlawful combatant'. Such a figure cannot be assimilated to that of the enemy soldier because terrorist organizations have not signed the Geneva Conventions and so the 'unlawful combatant' cannot be protected by them. The same goes for the combatant fighting for a 'rogue state' – for instance for the Taliban in Afghanistan. If they were instead 'criminals' who had committed crimes in times of peace, they would be protected by so-called habeas corpus. This commands anyone who takes a prisoner to justify their arrest and indicate when they will be released – 'you have your body' and your physical freedom will be restored to you. This was an order issued by English law as far back as the twelfth century, and since then it has been accepted as a principle of the inviolability of the individual human person. But the legislation in times of peace is not applicable in times of war. The 'war on terror', which is effectively a declaration of a state of exception, suspends habeas corpus and temporarily revokes national laws and international norms – indeed, for an indefinite period, which lasts as long as achieving the end goal takes. The 'unlawful combatant', the terrorist subject, can be transferred to some location distant from the law and tortured. That is how torture becomes a preventative measure.

It is not difficult to detect, within this para-legal bio-politics, the Schmittian trace which characterizes the very fundamentals of western democracy. For the Führer's *Kronjurist*, the boundary between friend and enemy is always unstable. He made this observation in his 1932 essay *The Concept of the Political*. The 'enemy' hides away and makes himself unrecognizable. It was no chance thing that Schmitt saw the Jew as paradigmatic of the 'enemy' par excellence. The task of politics is to use the faculties of the imagination to construct a recognizable face of the enemy. After the Cold War and the melting away of many age-old glaciers, the US political imagination pointed to the 'unlawful combatant' as the threatening and disturbing face of an 'enemy' who by definition lacks any positive legal status. In dealing with such an enemy, international law could thus be suspended.

The first 'unlawful combatants' were transferred to Guantánamo Bay in the aftermath of the invasion of Afghanistan. The US base in Cuba thus became a zone of non-law, together with many other detention sites of which we still do not have any detailed map, the most renowned of which is the Abu Ghraib prison in Iraq.

The strategy pursued by the US administration's *Kronjuristen* consists of two main themes: first, to show that these prisoners are 'unlawful combatants' and cannot be protected by international conventions; and second, to defend the legitimacy of subjecting them to 'coercive interrogation', which is not called 'torture' and which carries no risk of prosecution for the officials or agents carrying it out.

The turning point came with the so-called 'Torture Memo', written in response to public opinion's growing protests at the use of torture on prisoners. It was presented by John Yoo and Jay Bybee on 1 August 2002 in the name of the Office of Legal Counsel of the Department of Justice. Basing themselves on a specious interpretation of both the law and US military codes, the two *Kronjuristen* Yoo and Bybee acknowledged the acts of violence that had been perpetrated, but challenged the claim that they could be classed as 'torture'. They wrote that '[p]hysical pain amounting to torture must be equivalent in intensity to the pain accompanying serious physical injury, such as organ failure, impairment of bodily function, or even death'.[5] For it to be torture, it would have to be carried out with 'a specific intention' and leave obvious physical wounds. So in this view, waterboarding – i.e. simulated drowning – rape, the denial of food, water or medicine, or the use of electrodes (Greenberg 2006: 283–391) did not constitute torture.

But torture cannot magically be transformed into non-torture simply by altering the name. The formulation 'coercive interrogation' is a linguistic ruse through which the US administration has tried to legalize torture by narrowing its definition. Tellingly, the Military Commission Act adopted by the US Congress on 17 October 2006, ratifying Bush's order and establishing exceptional military tribunals for terrorist subjects, was widely termed the 'Torture Law'. On 12 June 2008, the US Supreme Court declared unconstitutional the 'special regime' which the Bush administration had established. As Matthew Alexander argued in an article on 20 January 2010 in the *New York Times*, although on 22 January 2009 Obama had signed an executive order to outlaw torture and close detention camps like Guantánamo, the problem did not seem to have been resolved. Interrogation policy continued to be 'inhumane and counterproductive'.

The Torture Memo and the measures taken after 9/11 contributed both to spreading torture and to weakening the shared prohibition against it. A taboo was broken, and the condemnation of torture no longer seemed self-evident nor taken for granted.

8   The debate over torture

No longer stigmatized and in part even rehabilitated, torture could thus become the subject of a wide and long-enduring public debate. It had freed itself of that gothic aura that had made it so obscene and fearsome over previous centuries. It was thus possible to openly speculate on the proper use of

[5] Memorandum for Alberto R. Gonzales Counsel to the President, 1 August 2002, now in Danner (2004: 115).

torture in exceptional cases. But even to accept a discussion of its use already put into question the on-principle refusal of torture, the absolute prohibition. This established the bases for what Luban (2014) has called the 'liberal ideology of torture', which has gradually come to assert itself.

The debate began in the press and the big TV stations like Fox, CNN and CBS within a few weeks of the attack on the Twin Towers. Not only did influential politicians take part in this debate, but so too did journalists, opinion-makers, intellectuals, jurists, philosophers and luminaries of the academic world. An article published by Jonathan Alter in *Newsweek* on 5 November 2001 had the telling title 'Time to Think about Torture', contending that this was a necessary response to terror. Yet the words that opened the debate also pointed to a democracy gone bankrupt. This was how Alter defended his position in favour of resorting to torture.

> We can't legalize physical torture; it's contrary to American values. But even as we continue to speak out against human-rights abuses around the world, we need to keep an open mind about certain measures to fight terrorism, like court-sanctioned psychological interrogation. And we'll have to think about transferring some suspects to our less squeamish allies, even if that's hypocritical. (Alter 2001: 45)

A few days later, on 8 November 2001, this was echoed in the *Los Angeles Times* by the renowned jurist Alan Dershowitz, professor of law at Harvard and a prominent figure on the US media stage. In his article 'Is there a Torturous Road to Justice?', he considered for the first time the possibility of a legal torture warrant (Dershowitz 2001).

A particularly decisive role in this debate went to the extreme hypothesis of a ticking time bomb, which could take many lives if it exploded. This is in fact a well-worn example, dating back at least as far as the Algerian War. Even in that period, Jean-Marie Le Pen, together with Jean-Maurice Demarquet – both founders of the *Front National des Combattants* – invoked this possibility. As they wrote in *Le Monde* on 27 May 1957: 'if it is necessary to torture one man to save a hundred, then torture cannot be avoided'. Later, Le Pen would openly state that he had carried out torture.[6] Vidal-Naquet addressed this argument in his book *Torture: Cancer of Democracy*, published in French in 1959, which for the first time reported on the use of torture by a democracy. The 'time-bomb' argument was subsequently adopted by German jurists (see Bahar 2009). The discussion was prompted by the September 2002 case of Jakob von Metzler, the 11-year-old son of a banker kidnapped by the law student Magnus Gäfgen. The latter, identified by the police as he came to pick up the ransom money, did not want to reveal the location where he was holding the boy. In reality, he had already killed him. Frankfurt's deputy police commissioner Wolfgang Daschner was convinced that there was still time to act, and he threatened Gäfgen with torture. He was then himself put on trial and sentenced. The case had a great deal of resonance in Germany and raised the question of *Rettungsfolter* – 'life-saving torture' – i.e. the ambiguous formulation with which the jurist Winfried Brugger emphasized torture's potentially redemptive capacity of protecting public safety (2005). But already in December 1992 the famous sociologist Niklas Luhmann had sought to undermine the absolute prohibition against torture by invoking the 'ticking time bomb' argument. During a lecture at Heidelberg University, he asked if 'there still exist irrevocable norms in our society' (1993). In Germany the response was steadfast (see Reemtsma 2005). But it could not be said that the echoes of this debate died down entirely.

A decisive contribution to the banalization of torture in the American debate came from images: not so much the ones in photographs and documentaries, but rather ones from the realms of film and fiction. These ranged from the TV series *24*, rightly labelled part of a newly invented genre of 'torture porn', to the 2006 James Bond film *Casino Royale* and the controversial 2012 film *Zero Dark Thirty*. Thus, over several years, the US public could enthusiastically follow the efforts of the hero-agent who tortures the terrorist for the common good. This was the spectacle of torture that made an act of squalor into an indispensable rite of passage on the way towards a greater humanity.

[6] See the interview with Le Pen in *Combat*, 9 November 1962.

9   The dilemma of 'getting our hands dirty': Thomas Nagel and Michael Walzer

If we want to understand the philosophical dimension and the political significance of the US debate, we need to look back far earlier than 9/11. We could say that it all began with an essay by Thomas Nagel, one of the most authoritative voices in American analytic philosophy. His *War and Massacre* was published in 1971 in the context of the Vietnam War, which lasted from 1961 to 1973. Nagel asked if there is a 'moral basis for the rules of war' and, most importantly, examined what 'conduct' should be adopted during military actions. Achieving a certain end could justify recourse to a means that one might otherwise wish to avoid. From this emerged a series of 'moral dilemmas'. Nagel contended:

> [Someone] may believe, for example, that by torturing a prisoner he can obtain information necessary to prevent a disaster, or that by obliterating one village with bombs he can halt a campaign of terrorism. If he believes that the gains from a certain measure will clearly outweigh its costs, yet still suspects that he ought not to adopt it, then he is in a dilemma produced by the conflict between two disparate categories of moral reason: categories that may be called *utilitarian* and *absolutist*. Utilitarianism gives primacy to a concern with what will *happen*. Absolutism gives primacy to a concern with what one is *doing*. (1972: 124)

While remaining as ambiguous as needed, Nagel criticized the 'absolutist' position, which he identified with pacifism and more generally with the perspective of those who stick intransigently to their principles, for instance, the position that maintains that it is wrong to kill in any circumstances and for any reason, regardless of what consequences follow from this. Killing another person is thus absolutely prohibited. The same goes for torture. Using a very dubious term which itself contains an inherent value-judgement, Nagel spoke of 'absolutism'. Conversely, the 'utilitarian' position is that assumed by those who want to 'maximise good and minimise evil', either at an individual level or by way of institutions. Nagel does not dwell on utilitarianism for, he tells us, it is 'simple' and has a 'natural appeal' (1972: 125). It is worth emphasizing that the two labels 'absolutist' and 'utilitarian' would each become entrenched, orienting the US debate. Nagel's intention was to make these the two poles of a moral dilemma. Who could ever be truly absolutist? For him, this position was utopian because it does not deal with the reality of wars and massacres; paradoxical because it can impose the demand to abstain from the lesser evil, with all the harm that results; and, ultimately, immoral because it allows the most terrible wrongdoing in the name of preserving its own purity. Apparently, Nagel was seeking some sort of mediation. Yet, on closer inspection, he puts so-called 'absolutism' on trial by making it a regulating ideal, both senselessly abstract and conveniently unrealizable; all the more so, in the sense that if it were ever realized, it would prove to be reprehensible. Here the principles of those who think we should never kill or torture seem to waver.

Nagel removed the absolute prohibition against killing and torture. This generated an ever more energetic and impetuous current which over subsequent years attempted to justify this practice. Without ever coming out in the open, Nagel was skilful in following an effective argumentative tactic often concealed by sophistry. First of all, he took the acceptance of war for a given. He thus projected a 'mortal conflict' in a war scenario, in which – with a further, far from self-evident move – he put forward his normative approach, passing it off as the best one possible. In this view, the only serious response was not to speculate on the big questions but to think about how to resolve problems – i.e. to answer the questions 'What should we do?', 'How should we behave?', 'How can we justify our choices?'

In this context, it is unsurprising that moral primacy was ascribed to utilitarianism, even if Nagel did not hide a certain lack of satisfaction with a perspective that could rush into the abyss of large-scale massacre unless it was held back by a barrier presented by some other principle. But in Nagel's eyes, the utilitarian has the merit of being immersed in the concreteness of action. The utilitarian not only calculates costs and benefits before making decisions but also takes responsibility for all the consequences. The utilitarian sacrifices himself and his ethics on the altar of the lesser evil. On the contrary, the absolutist, who wants to preserve his own moral purity without dirtying his hands – even putting his own concerns above other people's lives – could be painted as immoral.

In this view, the life-and-death conflict creates a moral dilemma for each of them. It is a dilemma for the utilitarian because he will always think that he has not precisely calculated the costs; and it is a dilemma for the absolutist because he struggles to convince himself that he has confronted the problem in a satisfactory way. But in so doing Nagel sets up a – very dubious – further blow against pacifist absolutism.

The tactic Nagel adopted has bequeathed us two questions: lesser evilism, and getting one's hands dirty. In various forms, these two are the hinges of the US debate about the more or less explicit argument that torture should be accepted and legitimized again.

It is no chance thing that Michael Walzer explicitly invokes Nagel's moral dilemma in an article first published in 1973, 'Political Action. The Problem of Dirty Hands'. Given the themes it addressed and the proposals it adopted, this article was in turn destined to become an essential reference point for anyone seeking to justify the exceptional recourse to torture. Known abroad as a philosopher and intellectual aligned to liberal positions, Walzer has in fact often backed neoconservative policies. In a theoretical framework that alludes to the theme – elaborated in later work – of 'just and unjust wars', Walzer anticipates the example of a ticking time bomb and provides specific recommendations.

The moral dilemma can be read politically in terms of the drama of 'dirty hands'. Walzer cites the eponymous play by Sartre in which the communist leader Hoederer exclaims:

How afraid you are to soil your hands! All right, stay pure! What good will it do? Why did you join us? Purity is an idea for a yogi or a monk. You intellectuals and bourgeois anarchists use it as a pretext for doing nothing. To do nothing, to remain motionless, arms at your sides, wearing kid gloves. Well, I have dirty hands. Right up to the elbows. I've plunged them in filth and blood. But what were you hoping for? Do you think you can govern innocently? (Sartre 1949: 21, translation altered)

Walzer's response is blunt: 'No, I don't think I could govern innocently' (2004 [1973]: 61). He recognizes that this is perhaps a commonplace on politics, a conventional preconception. No one can succeed in politics without dirtying their hands. And, anyway, who would want to be governed by an absolutist? There is no lack of examples to back up this argument. The most dramatic is that which recounts the case of a politician who has just been elected, who notwithstanding his own belief in peace has to confront the crisis of a prolonged colonial war that involves his country. He tries to start fresh negotiations, and to this end takes the first flight to the colony's capital, which lies in terrorist hands. He is then faced with his first difficult decision. The rebels' leader, who has been captured, knows – or, better, perhaps knows – where the bombs are located that could go off over the next twenty-four hours on the city periphery. He orders that the man be tortured in order to save the lives of those who might die in the explosions, although he is himself convinced that torture is wrong, abominable – not just sometimes but in all cases.

Paradoxically, from the politics of 'getting one's hands dirty', there emerges the new figure of the noble torturer. He resembles Augustine's 'melancholy soldier' (XXX: letter 93), who knows that he is fighting a just war but does not thereby forget what a terrible thing it is to kill. The torturer that Walzer describes is a man all by himself, who bears total responsibility, gets his hands dirty and chooses the lesser evil. He knows that he is committing a crime and takes the moral burden for it upon himself. He is culpable. But precisely for this reason he is a 'moral politician' which, in Walzer's understanding, sounds like an oxymoron. He takes the decision imposed by conditions of necessity and demanded by the emergency situation. In so doing, he transgresses political, ethical and legal principles; and he does this for the common good, in full and sincere awareness of his own unavoidable culpability. He is prepared to take individual responsibility for his actions with all their moral and criminal consequences. Only this noble torturer, beset by his own scruples, can be entrusted with the onerous task of deciding when it is necessary – in wholly exceptional circumstances, of course – to resort to torture (see Terestchenko 2008: 89 ff.).

Overriding the rules does not mean repudiating them, still less getting rid of them. The 'moral politician' is not unaware of the rules; rather, he recognizes them in all their normative force. At the very moment in which he suspends the rules, he also takes a closer look at them, indeed not without a certain bitterness at the fact that he has been compelled to override them. Only a politician of such high moral calibre should order the use of torture: as Walzer comments, we don't want 'just anyone' (1973: 64) doing so. The noble torturer is the one who has a moral notion of the evil that he is committing. Only then will good be protected and the law preserved in its integrity.

Conscious of his own guilt and certain that he will be convicted by the courts, this noble torturer is a tragic figure because he is caught in a moral dilemma whose seriousness he is fully aware of. He does not try to exculpate the evil itself – while it is necessary, it is nonetheless evil, and nothing can make it good. Since the rules are not themselves abolished, there is no subversion of values. In the noble torturer we can discern the traits of Machiavelli's prince. Indeed, Walzer himself brings this figure into play. Unable to rely on legal pretexts, ethical alibis or cost–benefit calculations, the 'moral politician' is all alone. He can only count on his own virtue, his own abilities, his own courage, as he takes a decision that appears strictly personal in character, even if it is also a political one. Only he will answer for it, take responsibility for it, facing up to all the consequences and even the verdict of a civil or military trial. Yet the boundary between what is allowed and what is forbidden, the observance of the law and its violation, will have been maintained.

The fact that this is an individual decision should also underline its exceptional character. That is why, according to Walzer, torture should indeed remain an illegal practice to which recourse is made in emergency situations. Only this will leave intact the rule of law, which will continue to convict for torture. The political scientist Henry Shue takes a similar position, writing:

An act of torture ought to remain illegal so that anyone who sincerely believes such an act to be the least available evil is placed in the position of needing to justify his or her act

morally in order to defend himself or herself legally. The
torturer should be in roughly the same position as someone
who commits civil disobedience. Anyone who thinks an act
of torture is justified should have no alternative but to convince a group of peers in a public trial that all necessary conditions for a morally permissible act were indeed satisfied.
(2004: 58)

As if we could draw some sort of comparison – even a distant
one – between civil disobedience and torture on the basis that
both are violations of the law. As if we could compare the
courage required of anyone who publicly refuses to obey a
rule that she considers unjust – and who takes on all the
consequences of this refusal – and the cowardice inherent in
the act of torture.

10   Alan Dershowitz and the 'torture warrant'

In the United States, the debate around torture has played
out not so much among conservatives as among those who
declare themselves 'liberal Democrats'. A notable case in
point is Alan Dershowitz, who consistently lays claim to the
'liberal' label while presenting himself as a champion of
human rights. But his is a prominent name in the current
debate. As we see on closer inspection, Dershowitz is a partisan of torture who has skilfully caught the mood of the
times and interpreted what the polls are saying. He thus gives
voice to a strong trend in US public opinion since 9/11. If the
terrorist excludes himself from any democratic contract, why
on earth should his rights be protected?

In 2002, Dershowitz published *Why Terrorism Works*,
a very controversial book in which he outlined the measures that have to be taken in order to combat terrorism.
The 'tragic choices' which a democracy has to make include
torture (2002: 105 ff.). Yet Dershowitz does not simply
say 'let's torture the terrorist'. Rather, in a later text in his
own defence, he irritatedly rejects the accusations and deni-
gration coming from those, for example, who called him
'Torquemada Dershowitz' in explicit reference to the famous

inquisitor. He insists that he was against torture, and that, if anything, he was just trying to find the means to limit it. So what is his position?

For Dershowitz, as for Walzer, torture is an evil that is unavoidable in exceptional circumstances, such as those produced by the 'war on terror'. The difference is that while one is Machiavellian, the other is utilitarian. Both, however, agree on this much: that it is not a question of discussing whether to make recourse to torture faced with the emergency of some extreme threat, but only of deciding in what manner to proceed. The tragic figure of the noble torturer departs in favour of a more impersonal 'torture warrant'. The term Dershowitz uses implies a judicial authorization, a legal guarantee.

Enough with the hypocrisy: torture is practised everywhere, more or less secretly, and not only by despotic and dictatorial regimes. It is pointless to deny it. Dershowitz is a realist – and he invokes the principle of realism. So it is time to recognize that democratic states torture. Perhaps it takes place behind the scenes, in democracy's dark patches, unknown to the ill-informed citizens. Yet it takes place with their complicity, however involuntarily. So it is better to admit the realities and to try to regulate torture so that it does not get out of hand and to prevent it from being abused. A legal warrant would resolve everything. So we have to request a judge's prior approval in order to avoid illegal excesses, and most importantly to allow for a broad 'public accountability' – and the key word is 'accountability'– in those few cases in which torture really is necessary.

For Dershowitz, too, the emblematic case – it is superfluous even to say it – is also the example of the ticking time bomb. Should the terrorist in the know about immediate attacks not, perhaps, be tortured? We need only a 'nonlethal torture', for instance 'a sterilized needle inserted under the fingernails to produce unbearable pain without any threat to health or life' (2002: 144). Moreover, if the death penalty is justified for murdering a single individual, why not accept non-lethal torture when this would prevent a massacre? All the more so, given that death is final whereas pain is only temporary.

With certain autobiographical overtones, Dershowitz repeatedly outlines the context in which he began to reflect on the difficulty of finding a compromise over civil liberties. It was in the 1980s, and he had just begun to work at the Hebrew University in Jerusalem. It is unsurprising that Israel is portrayed as the democracy most exposed to all the risks of terror. Indeed, it is for this reason that in the wider debate on the difficult balance between security and human rights, Israel appears as a cutting-edge laboratory. But for Dershowitz the decisive case is America – and not Israel, from whose choices he distances himself. Detailing further a theme that he addressed already in that period, he writes:

> if torture would, in fact be employed by a democratic nation under the circumstances, would the rule of law and principles of accountability require that any use of torture be subject to some kind of judicial (or perhaps executive) oversight (or control)? On this normative issue, I have expressed my views loudly and clearly. My answer, unlike that of the Supreme Court of Israel, is 'yes'. (Dershowitz 2004: 264)[7]

Dershowitz's argument revolves around two premises, in which empirical observations are mistaken for points of principle. The first of this pair is the principle of accountability. This consists of the idea that for a democracy to be a democracy, it must demand that the state's actions take place within the framework set out by law and overseen by public control. Assuming that the state does indeed carry out torture, it must therefore do it in a legal way; and it must not be a policeman or an agent of the CIA or FBI who decides, but rather a judge or an authority. The second is the more commonplace principle of the 'exception' represented by the ticking time bomb. This is the case in which torture can be chosen as the lesser evil.

While torture is a morally unjustifiable, it here becomes a politically legitimate and legally sound practice. Taking this approach, Dershowitz is even able to present himself as an opponent of torture, who is just trying to moderate its use. Yet in his dubious hyperrealism, he in fact justifies torture,

---

[7] On the position taken by Israel's Supreme Court, see section 17.

and, for the first time since the period of the Enlightenment, openly calls for its legalization. So we can understand why his argument has sparked uproar and been the target of numerous sharp critiques. Besides his sophisms, his specious reasoning and the errors in his argument – and there are more than a few – it is necessary to emphasize the points he makes that are simply unacceptable.

First of all, perhaps because he is immersed in the US context, Dershowitz seems to forget that after the Second World War the international community banned torture – with no exceptions. With his harangue for legalized torture, he sets himself against international law, tramples on human rights and undermines the very idea of the rule of law. It should not go unremarked that in his discourse the law gives in to the state, capitulating to a practice that it has never authorized, when it ought instead be the state that subjects itself to the law. And this is not just any practice. Law changes and adapts over time; it moves with the course of history. But it stops when faced with the inalienable principles standing at the base of human dignity, which are not up for negotiation.

Then there are a series of more specific questions. Who can guarantee that the particular case will not become a precedent that tears holes in the general rule and ultimately overwhelms it? Will judges be found who are up to the task and prepared to take on the burden of this warrant – perhaps even having to answer for their decision before a tribunal? Who will the criminal responsibility then fall on – those who do the torture, those who oversee it or those who give authorization for it?

But there is more. In what Dershowitz proposes, the evil is exculpated by necessity: since torture is a necessary evil, it transforms into a good. Here we see how he stands apart from Walzer. Even if Dershowitz repeatedly speaks of a 'moral difficulty', there is no difficulty for his morality, which is founded on a wholly utilitarian cost–benefit analysis. It is not by chance that he invokes Jeremy Bentham. In this context, it is impossible to do the wrong thing. For the whole question relies on a rational, objective, impersonal and neutral calculation. Who decides is removed from the ethical dilemma, the political *aut aut* ('either this or that'). Even faced with the ticking time bomb scenario, the calculated decision to act in the interest of the many can only lead to a positive outcome, which stands above dispute. This is now not even a lesser evil, but a good and just decision. The calculation itself dictates as much. Any scruples of conscience, any tragic doubts, now fade away. We are here far from Machiavelli, for whom being forced to penetrate – so to say – evil does not mean losing awareness that this is an evil, or still less, to paint it as good. Dershowitz, conversely, wipes away the always precarious boundary between good and evil. The heinous action which morality demands and approves, considering it the only possible response, suddenly reveals itself to be a good action. So there is no surprise that the law can be overridden, if calculation demands as much.

This economy of action leaves no room for personal responsibility. So the political space of the decision is reduced. If we can calculate what is better, or less bad, then what is the advantage of questioning it ourselves or with others? What sense does it make to reflect, and thus to deliberate, with all the anxious hesitation this entails? The certainty that comes with calculation eliminates any qualms that this might be an error. The judge figure, the warrant-giver as proposed by Dershowitz, is seen, in this light, as the impartial authority who is able accurately to calculate if, when, where and in what measure to proceed. He prevents excesses but also takes the burden off everyone else. Dershowitz prefers the expert to the noble torturer. From time to time the expert licenses the torture warrant, and in so doing also appears to shine the light that will guarantee transparency. This allows the accountability without which democracy would be unimaginable.

If this is how things are, and if the torture warrant does indeed respond to the demands of accountability – the idea of public responsibility that is at the very heart of political liberalism – then this means that liberal democracy can live with torture. The really important thing is the principle of public control, the obligation to be accountable for action. After all, for the exponents of Anglophone liberalism, this is the foundation of democracy. So the torture warrant would not then be a scandal, on condition, that is, that it is exercised according to the rules and employed against those who threaten order and violate the contract. In sum, torture would then be compatible with liberalism.

11   The lesser evil is still an evil

Whether explicitly or otherwise, the theory that is needed if
'exceptions' are to be made and the use of torture legitimized
is the morality of the 'lesser evil'. The fundamental idea, here,
is that we cannot choose between good and evil, but only
between one evil and a worse one. This is all the more true
in a context defined by global terror. So anti-terrorism policy
must first and foremost avoid the trap of so-called 'moral
purism'; the demand to protect human rights always and
everywhere.

Michael Ignatieff offers what is in many ways a paradigmatic theory of the lesser evil. He is a historian, essayist and
front-rank liberal politician, although in recent years his star
has rather waned. Indeed, his views on torture have themselves been openly challenged. Ignatieff sees torture as 'the
most complex case' that faces the ethics of the lesser evil. This
is because torture raises all the dilemmas that a liberal society
has to confront in a war against terrorism (Ignatieff 2004:
138–43). Although he distances himself from the arguments
of those like Dershowitz who want to bring the law into the
interrogation room, Ignatieff attempts to steer a 'middle
course' between the absolutist protection of human rights and
the pragmatism that is prepared to apply violent measures
for the sake of successful outcomes. This third position is the
outcome of a precarious balancing act. It results from the
clear-sighted choice of the lesser evil: 'it might be worth subjecting an individual to relentless – though non-physical –
interrogation to elicit critical information' (2004: 8). Such is
the 'ethics of emergency' formulated by Ignatieff. But what
is the dividing line between intensive interrogation and
torture? And who can guarantee that torture, which is formally repudiated, will not be accepted anew in a novel and
less obvious guise? Ignatieff recognizes this problem, albeit
without changing his position – which does not, therefore,
seem so far from the position upheld by the partisans of
torture. To back up his position, he makes recourse to the
theme of the lesser evil. 'Acts of justified violence', i.e. 'lesser
evils', are necessary in order to defend liberal democracy. This
argumentation consists of two crucial points: first, evil is

measurable, as greater and lesser evil; and second, that there is no escape from evil as such. We then opt for the lesser evil – while remaining conscious that this is an evil – only as a last resort and as necessity demands. For Ignatieff, there are no idyllic alternatives: 'Either we fight evil with evil or we succumb'(2004: 19). It is then worth asking if, in this oh-so realist description, liberalism does not end up appearing as the universe in which we respond to evil with evil and in which, most importantly, good does not reside. Is there some tragic bind that ties liberalism to evil?

Seeking to corroborate his position, Ignatieff invokes Arendt, for whom avoiding evil means thinking for oneself. He refers to the philosopher's reflection on civil disobedience. And yet it is precisely by citing Arendt that we can refute the theory of lesser evil, stripping it of any pretence to morality. She explains:

> In [this] moral justification, the argument of the lesser evil has played a prominent role. If you are confronted with two evils, thus the argument runs, it is your duty to opt for the lesser one, whereas it is irresponsible to refuse to choose altogether. Those who denounce the moral fallacy of this argument are usually accused of a germ-proof moralism which is alien to political circumstances, of being unwilling to dirty their hands; and it must be admitted that it is not so much political or moral philosophy (with the sole exception of Kant, who for this very reason frequently stands accused of moralistic rigorism) but religious thought that most unequivocally has rejected all compromises with lesser evils. Thus the Talmud holds, as I was told during a recent discussion of these matters: if they ask you to sacrifice one man for the security of the community, don't surrender him; if they ask you to give one woman to be ravished for the sake of all women, don't let her be ravished. . . . Politically, the weakness of the argument has always been that those who choose the lesser evil forget very quickly that they chose evil. (Arendt 2003: 35)

We should moreover add that the lesser evil always entails what Ignatieff himself defines as a 'moral hazard'. Torture itself clearly shows this, for it exposes whoever practises it to a very grave moral hazard – starting with the agents and public officials of democratic states. The torturer is not left unscathed by the violence that he inflicts on others.

12   *24*: the gentleman torturer

Much more influential on public opinion than the arguments
made by philosophers or articles by journalists is the TV
series *24*, produced by Fox. The protagonist is Jack Bauer,
an agent of the Los Angeles Counter Terrorism Unit. He is
the epic hero of a pop-drama that has enchanted millions of
viewers. He is the substitute for the missing political leader
whom we would have liked to have had in the post-9/11
world.

The series hit the screens on 6 November 2001, around
two months after the 9/11 attacks. The first episode, which
portrays a terrorist who attempts to blow up an aeroplane in
order to assassinate the Democrat candidate for the White
House, the African-American David Palmer, had, however, in
fact been filmed prior to the attacks, and much of the plot
had been outlined with disturbing foresight. Jack Bauer operates in a world riven with extreme danger. Everything revolves
around the imminence of a biological or nuclear terrorist
attack which threatens to be a cosmic catastrophe, the ultimate conflagration.

The show adopts a real-time narrative technique. Every
series consists of 24 hours, corresponding to the 24 hours of
Jack Bauer's day. The seconds and minutes pass on screen
relentlessly. The dominant theme of this political thriller is
emergency. It keeps the viewers in suspense and enthrals them
with its rushes of adrenaline. Yet even amidst the dramatic
events, the message is reassuring. The agent Jack Bauer is
identified as a providential and resolute figure, the fearless
avenger who sacrifices himself in order to save humanity.

How should we respond to terror? In *24*, the political
and moral dilemmas of this new era are portrayed in a tangible way. Reduced to an intensely personal level, they take
on unprecedented force. Perhaps no philosophical argument
could have achieved as much. This makes it even more perverse and harmful in effect. The realistic tone of this fictional drama immerses the spectator in real-time action, and
thus prevents her from keeping the necessary distance. Who
wouldn't be on Jack's side as he defends good against evil – at
any cost? Because Bauer, unlike predecessors such as James

Bond, is politically incorrect, puts two fingers up to the rules, transgresses norms and breaks with procedures. How else could he defeat evil, faced with such an emergency? Unyielding bureaucrats, corrupt politicians and shadowy conspirators are just so many obstacles to be overcome in the interests of fighting the omnipresent terrorist threat.

24's hero necessarily overrides the law and leaves aside moral conventions so that he can fulfil his patriotic duty and defend freedom. He is prepared to get his hands dirty. Anyone who faults his behaviour or cavils about his methods is either naive or simply unwilling to act to stop the nation's enemies. 'Let Jack get on with it!' – that is what we are meant to shout at the screen as we watch the series. For he is loyal, has shrewd intuition and always knows the right decisions to make even, and most importantly, in the extreme case of the ticking time bomb.

'America wants the war on terror fought by Jack Bauer. He's a patriot,' declared the series's co-writer Joel Surnow (Mayer 2007). Bauer represents a long tradition extending from action movies to westerns, celebrating the myth of the lone hero who fights evil from outside the system in the uncharted territory that opens up beyond the frontier. It is no surprise that the counter-terrorism agent enjoys enormous popularity, even in the academic world; that his actions are imitated by US soldiers; and, indeed, that the series is taken as a sort of manual – or that even conferences and meetings dedicated to the terror threat repeat the mantra 'What would Jack Bauer do?'

13   A political theology of torture

Concealed in the seductive and fearsome allure exerted by this figure is a secret that is none too difficult to unveil. Jack Bauer reminds us of Carl Schmitt's sovereign. He is the 'Decider' who suspends the law as he confronts the crisis. 'Sovereign is he who decides on the exception,' Schmitt writes in his 1922 work *Political Theology* (2005: 5). Jack Bauer goes beyond the boundaries of the law and places himself above it. But the paradox is that the agent in 24 decides what the exception is – and this is the theme of the show – in order to defend liberalism, whereas for Schmitt liberalism is itself the target. That is the goal in whose interests Jack Bauer carries out torture. He does so in every episode in order to extract vital information from the suspects: through sensory deprivation, drugging them, electrocution, simulated execution and so on. He does it to protect liberal society – obviously. And the torture in turn appears an obviously realist decision.

We can thus say that 24 is the film version of the liberal vision of torture that some US philosophers have helped to spread. Slavoj Žižek points an accusing finger at this attempt to banalize and normalize torture, as if it were unavoidable given the terrorist emergency. The series ought not to be underestimated or taken as simply an entertaining piece of television. There can be no doubt as to its performative power: dilemmas are not only portrayed but answered. We proceed beyond the suspension of ethical norms towards an utter bonfire of ethics. How, otherwise, would it be possible to present this extreme violence as an ordinary act carried out by normal people?

This is the reason why Žižek speaks of Jack Bauer as a 'Himmler in Hollywood' (2006). Here he is making explicit reference to the theme of the banality of evil, as addressed by Arendt. More particularly, the question that the Bauer character puts back on the table is none other than 'Himmler's dilemma'; how do you make an individual do dirty work without them becoming a monster? For it is easy to conduct a noble act for one's homeland; it is rather more difficult to commit a crime. And, as we learn from Himmler, a fervent reader of the *Bhagavad Gita*, acting at a distance is sufficient to keep one from being wholly complicit. The ethical catastrophe of the Nazi executioners was precisely their capacity to remain normal, even as they carried out the most heinous of crimes.

For Žižek, such a perverse normality resurfaces not only in 24 but in the whole US debate on torture. Dershowitz's argument should be turned on its head: it is not a matter of proving to be more or less hypocritical. Rather, the question is: to what benefit is it being said – why talk about it? To popularize something is never neutral. For Žižek, the problem of 24 lies less in its content than in the fact that it makes torture public, and in the last analysis, legitimizes it.

Against liberal Dershowitz's honesty, we should therefore paradoxically stick to the apparent 'hypocrisy': OK, we can well imagine that in a specific situation, confronted with the proverbial 'prisoner who knows' and whose words can save thousands, we would resort to torture, even (or, rather, precisely) in such a case, however, it is absolutely crucial that we do not elevate this desperate choice into a universal principle; following the unavoidable brutal urgency of the moment, we should simply do it. Only in this way, in the very inability or prohibition to elevate what we had to do into a universal principle, do we retain the sense of guilt, the awareness of the inadmissibility of what we have done. (Žižek 2002: 103)

By no means is Žižek here justifying the use of torture, as some believe. Instead, he is contending that while we cannot rule out that a 'desperate choice' will present itself, this single case must not become normalized. Notwithstanding our response to Jack Bauer, it is indispensable that we protect and maintain our horror against torture.

Jack Bauer's tragic greatness and noble sense of self-sacrifice shows torture in a new light. It suddenly appears not only necessary but even redemptive. A political theology of torture takes shape, almost a soteriology for a time of terror. It is the torturer who liberates us from evil. Wholly transformed, he is no longer the wicked jailer, the ruthless and cruel executioner, but rather the charismatic agent, honest and loyal, resigned to the fate that is bearing down on him, and yet managing not to give in. Bauer opposes blind fanaticism with cold pragmatism and the awareness that – despite everything – he will always be in the right. 'Do you understand the difference between dying for something and dying for nothing? The only reason I fought so hard to stay alive . . . was because I didn't want to die for nothing. Today I can die for something. My way, my choice.' Nothing can stop him: not rivalries, nor tricks, nor bitterness, nor grief. Isolated, betrayed, and ever more an outsider in a world where there is no one left to trust, Bauer maintains his unshakeable sense of duty. And in combating the terrorist plots he is ready to sacrifice himself, to torture himself and to be tortured. He drugs himself in order to infiltrate a narco-trafficking ring, fakes his own death and agrees to be handed over to a distant dictatorship by his own government in order to languish in prison there. He is the suffering servant of the American people. But he is not granted a redeeming death. Each time he picks himself up, only to plunge once again into the theatre of evil.

The torturer is tortured – the sovereign succumbs to the sovereignty of torture. Seemingly himself a sacrificial victim, Jack Bauer is no less than his victims a *homo sacer*. Indeed, he has ventured into the shadowy space of an outlaw, where all he does is what is right and necessary in order to defeat terror. That means torturing terrorists and also suspects – those who have ties to the terrorists, the agents who are and are not colluding with them. In this space, Bauer is also exposed; he, too, is at the mercy of torture. So he may himself be tortured, even killed, without anyone having to answer for this, or being punished. For in the eyes of the law – the pure form that he has himself left behind – Jack Bauer's life is now valueless. That is why he can anonymously disappear into that vacuum of law's dominion in which it is as if he had never existed.

What redeems Bauer, then, is torture itself. This is the agent's terrible faith. Redemptive and purifying, torture appears as the ultimate encapsulation of the 'war on terror', which demands an extreme yet unacknowledged sacrifice. In the apocalyptic scenario that takes shape in the backdrop to *24*, there thus remains nothing but a soteriology of torture.

It is hard to understand how this ought to be combined with democracy, or still less defend democracy. But without doubt Jack Bauer shows the close connection between torture and terror. Moreover, in *24* the dilemmas posed soon dissolve in the face of straightforward responses and simple solutions. The utilitarian calculation leaves no room for doubt. Notwithstanding its much-praised realism, in exploiting fears and indulging hopes Fox's fictional drama promises an illusory impunity and spreads a profoundly amoral morality centred on the sacrifice that saves one's own life and the lives of others.

14   Why not torture the terrorist? The ticking time bomb

A terrorist has been captured. He is suspected of having set a time bomb in one of the city's many schools. A lot of

children are in class at this very moment. It is impossible to
try to carry out a rapid evacuation of the schools. Immediately subjected to interrogation, conducted by legal means,
the man has refused to give answers. Time is pressing. The
bomb could explode at any moment. Dozens, hundreds of
human lives are at risk. Would it not be appropriate to use a
certain pressure – more psychological than physical – to get
him to give out valuable information? In such circumstances,
isn't it necessary to resort to – non-lethal – torture?

The immediate response is 'yes!' Who could respond otherwise? And in general that is the position of those who are
called upon to take one, faced with the scenario of the ticking
time bomb. We can change the narrative, add or take away
certain elements and make it hyperbolically more dramatic,
airing the possibility that the presumed terrorists are on the
verge of unleashing a germ attack or are even in possession
of nuclear weapons.

In any case, it here becomes impossible to respond with a
sharp 'no'. Thus torture can be considered a legitimate
weapon in the age of global terrorism. The call to legalize
torture, even while we acknowledge its immorality, rests on
precisely this case – the scenario of the ticking time bomb.
From Baghdad to Madrid, from London to Sharm el Sheikh,
from Beirut to Istanbul, we have lost count of the bombs that
have, lamentably, been primed and exploded in public spaces,
massacring defenceless victims.

So it should be no surprise that the time-bomb scenario
has been taken very seriously by American philosophers – not
only by the neocons but also by liberals. As Bob Brecher
observes in his book dedicated to this question: Dershowitz
'is not alone' in 'what is often called the "new realism" about
torture' (2007: 6). In this regard, we only need cite Martha
Nussbaum: 'I don't think any sensible moral position would
deny that there might be some imaginable situations in which
torture [of a particular individual] is justified' (see Press
2003). By 'sensible moral position', she means the *a priori*
repudiation of torture. The principle seems to fall to pieces
under the blows of hard reality. And is this not, perhaps, the
fate of all principles and all a prioris? Faced with the blind
fanaticism of terrorism, which threatens innocent lives,
morality and law do not seem to hold; they thus have to be
revisited. The ethical purism of beautiful souls is forced to

give in to the facts. Unless, that is, it wants to compete with the terrorists to see who is more fanatical. The universal condemnation of torture, written into western culture in the wake of the Second World War, ratified by international treaties, would thus no longer be defensible, nor acceptable, in practice. Who could ever doubt the need to resort to coercive interrogation if so many lives rely on this? Then we have to recognize that in conditions of necessity like those proposed by the ticking time-bomb scenario, for which even the penal codes of many democratic countries would accept a suspension of the law, torture would be inevitable. If anything, the important thing is to control and regulate it.

The terrorist emergency is forcefully bearing down on us. The key thing is that this is an exceptional case. The ticking time-bomb dilemma risks bringing down the whole edifice of human rights and undermining the principles won at such great difficulty over the centuries – the ideas that only yesterday seemed irreversibly accepted beginning, for example, with the assumption that a prisoner's body is inviolable. The ticking time-bomb story renders acceptable the hypothesis that the state will torture, or rather that state torture will become legal in some exceptional circumstances – and this in a society bearing the stamp of democratic liberalism.

We must admit that the ticking time-bomb dilemma has a piercing force; given its obvious political and ethical repercussions, it cannot be underestimated. On closer inspection, it does not allow any dispute. The doves fall silent, and the purist 'idealists' who always and everywhere defend human dignity, are forced to abandon their strongest convictions and give up the stage to the hawks, the pragmatic 'realists'. For it is these latter who are able to maintain a resolute focus on what is best for the greatest number, to calculate costs and benefits, to measure up the consequences, to prevent the catastrophe and secure a certain success.

Such a distressing scenario brings to mind the countless images of terrorist attacks that have been reproduced on the big screen. But it does not relate the experience of any one attack in particular or seem to correspond to any situation that has really taken place. The hypothetical character of the whole dilemma reminds us instead rather more of 24, the series wholly constructed around the plot of the ticking time bomb. Does this hypothesis not, then, consist of the same supposed 'realism' as 24 – which is to say, the same fiction? If this were indeed true, then the debate on the ticking time bomb that has unfolded in America, involving philosophers and intellectuals, engaging media and public opinion, and also bearing on the political world – offering a possible seal of approval for the choices taken as part of the 'war on terror' – would prove to revolve around a mere fable. Indeed, it is a fable brandished as somehow more real than reality itself. Can we really make political decisions of such serious ethical charge on the basis of a fiction, an imaginary representation? In philosophy, can we resort to unreal tales, and then on this fictional basis purport to edify a new and more realistic ethics, adequate to the terror threat? Unless, that is, the fable is just an ideological pretext. Across its countless and differing versions, the ticking time-bomb scenario appears to be a product of fantasy. When we pay closer attention to the 'facts' related in this scenario, we see that they are not even plausible. The entire situation is constructed on improbable and absurd presuppositions.

We need only mention a few of these: it is assumed that the authorities are aware of an imminent attack; that they have captured one of the terrorists who has set the bomb; that this terrorist really has the necessary information; that there is no effective means of making him talk other than torture; that there are no other possible means of saving human life; that the torture will be effective, and because the terrorist will not have some plan B he will speak the truth.

We could go on pulling apart the logical and rhetorical structure of this story. Why on earth would it be desirable in this situation of imminent catastrophe – in which military strategists, political leaders and the apologists of torture speak of 'necessity' – to subject the suspected terrorist to the long and uncertain praxis of coercive interrogation, i.e. non-lethal torture? Or perhaps it would be more opportune to make recourse to the proven, old methods of traditional torture. Moreover, we should expect that the terrorist who has planned an attack – assuming this is indeed our man – would be ready to die; he would then have no difficulty in resisting torture, or better, providing wrong information. From the US Army Field Manual (KUBARK 1963: 34–52) to

Augustine's reflection on the presumption of innocence in his
work *City of God* (XIX: 6), there is total agreement on the
unreliability of confessions extracted under torture.

The examples usually adopted to corroborate the ticking
time-bomb dilemma have always been disproved. The most
famous is the one invoked by Dershowitz and many others:
the case of Abdul Hakim Murad. In 1995, during an imposing security operation, the Philippine National Police discov-
ered the plans that had been set out by Murad, an al-Qaeda
member who was preparing a series of attacks against seven
passenger aircraft heading towards the Pacific. According
to the version popularized after 9/11, as support for torture
grew in the United States, the Filipino police subjected Murad
to 67 days of beatings, waterboarding, psychological violence, stubbing out cigarettes on his genitalia and threatening
sexual violence. Murad broke and confessed his plot, which
would have cost the lives of four thousand passengers. This
episode was meant to demonstrate how rational and effective torture is. 'What would have happened if Murad had
been in American custody?', historian Jay Winik thundered
in the columns of the *Wall Street Journal*. Many echoed his
claims. The famous columnist Jonathan Alter commented that
'[s]ome torture clearly works' (Alter 2001; Winik 2001). But
in reality, the facts played out very differently; 'the Manila
police got all the important information from Murad in the
first few minutes, when they seized his laptop' (McCoy 2007:
112). Subsequently, during the weeks of torture, Murad
added only a few details as he tried to put an end to the pain
of torture. These were but the superfluous, feeble confirma-
tions of the conjecture that the police had been suggesting
to him.

Similar, though less striking, are other thwarted attacks,
such as those that Scotland Yard and the British security
services uncovered on 10 August 2006, thanks to classic
investigative techniques. Up until the arrest of the suspects,
the security services were unaware that an attack was imminent. Here, imminence is confused with probability. For
anyone other than those who are actually planning it, an
attack is an unexpected event, impossible to predict. That is
not to say that we should not try to prevent it. But the ticking
time-bomb scenario would have us believe that we can keep

attackers and attacks under control and that torture is an indispensable means for achieving this.

Only by torturing the terrorist can we deactivate the bomb and stop time. So it does not matter if we ask – as a matter of necessity – for the torture of just one person to be set against the very unpredictable prospect of many people dying. In the 'economic model' of torture, numbers count (see Wisnewski and Emerick 2009: 16–45). It is precisely this utilitarian principle that is meant to provide ethical legitimacy for torture. But what then can we say about the person doing the torturing? A terrorist is a terrorist – he is not a citizen, nor a soldier; he does not respect the law or the rules of war. He sets himself outside any political contract, but also – for this same reason – outside any human bond. Reciprocity no longer holds in his case. Always and only identified with the action he carries out, consigned to an anonymous and chilling hostility, for the terrorist there can be no empathy nor human sympathy. Why, then, not torture the terrorist?

We should turn the ticking time-bomb argument on its head, as Luban suggests, reformulating it in the following way:

> If the only way to get a terrorist to reveal the location of the ticking bomb is to torture you – that's right, you, the audience member, personally, for days on end – do you think the government should do it? You'll be kidnapped, hooded, have your clothes cut off; you'll be diapered and dressed in an orange jumpsuit, blindfolded, shot up with sedative, flown to Cuba, beaten, stripped naked and mocked by members of the opposite sex, hogtied, blasted with ear-splitting rap music and strobe lights for hours, hosed down and thrown into a frigid cell overnight, then shackled to an eye-bolt in the floor and made to stand up until your ankles double in size and your kidneys start to fail. Then you'll be chained to the ceiling with your arms behind your back, and lastly have sterilized needles thrust under your fingernails. For some reason or other, that's the only thing that will make the terrorist talk. Should we do it?' (Luban 2014: 94)

Torture is an emotive form of counter-terrorism that responds to terror with terror. But in the ticking time-bomb dilemma, torture is not stigmatized as brutal violence; it is presented as an action incumbent upon us, imposed by the calculation of the lesser evil and dictated by necessity. Whether it is the noble torturer, the utilitarian or Jack Bauer who carries it out, torture appears the only option if we are to avoid imminent catastrophe. It appears to be so. But it is not and never has been this.

Ruchama Marton, founder of Israel's Physicians for Human Rights, has intervened on the question. She contends that even the most aggressive torture has never helped to deactivate a bomb. 'Anyway', she asks, 'how long is it ticking? Is it going off in ten minutes, or two hours, or three weeks? In reality, there is no such thing as a clear case of the ticking bomb' (see Salomon 2001).

The ideology of legalized torture is built on mere fable. Based on historical experience, we see that the ticking time-bomb scenario has never played out in reality, which supposes that it is a wholly improbable scenario. So we should reject not only the conclusions that the argument wishes to draw but also the hypothesis itself. For the trap lies in presenting a particular case that would change the whole question if it were empirical evidence, when in fact it has never actually occurred. On closer inspection, this 'realism' is pseudo-realism. And the exception that would supposedly justify torture proves to be a fictitious hypothesis, not deduced from facts but instead forged from fantasy. The empirical reasoning drawn from the fiction examines concrete circumstances, and thus gradually becomes enriched with detail. We are sucked into a dizzying spiral of minute analyses, of unsolvable dilemmas, where we lose sight of the question itself. Intoxicated by this pseudo-realism, we end up almost accepting that torture is indeed necessary in this crisis.

If the ticking bomb argument plays on our visceral impulses and emotions, confronting us with a heinous threat, it also introduces an artificially transparent world in which certainties dominate, where evil is calculable, where everything can be articulated as a logical sequence where the right decisions assert themselves at each moment, despite the implacable urgency.

The dilemma is not a dilemma. The apparent complexity of this more or less specious reasoning ends up as an intellectual game, a piece of quasi-entertainment that distracts us from the real question. And using the alibi of emergency, it risks passing off institutionalized torture as something obviously necessary. That is why the ticking time-bomb scenario is nothing but an imposture, a deceit, a powerful propaganda tool.

15   Dangerous, pseudo-philosophical tales

The fable of the terrorist who has planted a time bomb somewhere and may therefore be tortured by the police is one of a series of dilemmas that has distracted the attention of analytical moral philosophy in recent years. The most famous is the trolley problem, originating in an article published by the British philosopher Philippa Foot in 1967. We can summarize this dilemma as follows.

An out-of-control railway trolley is heading at full speed towards five men tied to the tracks. You are on an overpass from which you can observe the impending tragedy. But there is a fat man, a stranger, standing next to you. If you push him onto the tracks, his body will block the trolley. So even if he dies as a result, five lives will be saved. So would you kill the fat man?

We might find it hard to believe that a whole 'trolleyology' consisting of academic exercises and board games (see Edmonds 2013) could have developed on this basis. 'Why me?', one might reply. 'Why am I on the overpass? Why is it up to me to choose between two evils?' And this is indeed an appropriate response, for there is a sleight of hand hidden behind the 'you', which seeks immediately to draw the interlocutor in. It is a sleight of hand because I would never find myself in that situation and because, upon closer inspection, the dilemma between the two evils suggests an ethical transgression. Whether I push the fat man off, or allow the five on the tracks to be hit, in both cases I will be the murderer. This is analogous to the ticking time-bomb scenario, where we are summoned to decide whether we should allow a hundred people to be killed or else torture the terrorist.

The worldview that these tales bring to light is that of a cartoonish world where we inevitably choose between evil and evil, with a greater and lesser evil that can be quantified through a utilitarian calculation of costs and benefits. More than an ethic of capitalism, this is a capitalism of ethics. And what is also impressive is the moral void that it presents. These fables appear realistic, and yet they are wholly fictitious and abstract. They would have us believe that our existence is a laboratory in which each person can experiment with the most absurd hypotheses, using elucubrations and argumentative games, without too much risk. What does it matter if these are questions of life and death? Everything is banalized in a game-like version of ethics, which, we ought to recognize, has little ethical about it.

Moral dilemmas of this kind are comparable to logical analyses of propositions. They can be allowed as classroom exercises, but they become inadmissible as soon as they are applied to reality. The trolley problem is a sophist's dilemma that seeks to trap us in the constricted and tragic position of choosing between two crimes. We should reject not only the solutions but the question itself. To get bogged down in disputes and dissertations on the trolley problem, as this neuro-economy does, is a legitimate enough pastime, however idle, despite the fact that it is not wholly innocuous. But it cannot become the servant of moral conscience. For it imposes an authoritarian *aut aut* – kill or allow others to be killed, torture or allow others to be massacred – which is not the experience of those who have to make the choice. If that were so, then this would have very grave consequences. The torture example itself shows the danger inherent in these pseudo-philosophical stories, which could become a powerful means of political manipulation.

16   Illegitimacy: the torturer state

What is new in the first stretch of the twenty-first century is that a democratic state can remain democratic, even if it allows torture within its borders or goes so far as to legalize it. What had been unthinkable except under dictatorial regimes now takes place in democracies. These latter can assume totalitarian attitudes, albeit without – apparently – changing their political order. We cannot, however, avoid asking what the consequences of this unprecedented phenomenon are. What does it mean for a democratic state to allow institutionalized torture?

In order to shed light on this latest boundary, it is worth examining the contrast between two visions of 'democracy': on the one hand, a pragmatic vision that seeks to ensure government by the majority and to protect the formal means of public deliberation; and on the other hand, an ethical vision, more concerned with protecting human rights and the dignity of each individual person, as concretized in the possibility of articulating the form of one's own life. These two visions can coexist and do not necessarily contradict one another. But faced with the terrorist emergency, the contrast between them becomes sharper, and the relationship breaks up.

The pragmatic vision of an Anglophone bent sees the principle of public oversight as the linchpin of the rule of law. Hence the ideal of accountability; the duty to explain one's reasoning, almost as an infinite process of self-justification; the continual need to impose rules and laws; the myth of transparency; and the obsession with information. Without doubt, such public oversight, impossible in any authoritarian regime, does have the virtue of nourishing dissent and keeping alive the ferment of democracy. In this context, however, 'democratic' appears to be synonymous with 'public'. For the exponents of US liberalism, democracy is not immediately bound up with inalienable human rights, but rather it is tied to the idea of the contract, to which everyone has supposedly freely signed up, and the consent that is time and again reproduced thanks to the deliberation over the rules of the game. For instance, it is worth referring to the thinking of John Rawls (2001). What counts in a fair society that aspires to public justice is mutuality, i.e. reciprocal obligations. It is impossible to grant constitutional guarantees to those who set themselves outside of that reciprocity, breaking the contract, for they have already ventured into a space that is simultaneously both outside reason and outside democracy, and it is impossible to extend the rights that respond to the ethical imperative without setting any conditions. We understand why torture – which has proven not to be incompatible with liberalism – tests the idea of a democracy that prioritizes public oversight, rather than one concentrated on human rights. In this context, the problem of the institutionalization of torture emerges. Who could deny that sincerity is better than hypocrisy? Yet it is naive to believe – not only in politics, but also in philosophy – that there is some field of truth counterposed to the field of lies, and that the correct choice will make itself unequivocally self-evident. According to such a rationalist and scientistic interpretation of the public sphere, transparency is always a value worth seeking while the secret inhabits a dark, intolerable recess which must be exposed to the light of day. We could say a lot more about this way of understanding secrecy. But the important thing is that in a simplistic view of democracy, not without certain Manichean traits, a consensus develops that we can even call for the legalization of the ethically unjust and unacceptable – for instance, torture. For as in Dershowitz's proposal, and also the proposal advanced by the famous federal judge Richard A. Posner (2006) – a leading exponent of the 'economics of law' – it would be under the public authorities' oversight.

Making the unjust legal has consequences not only for ethics but also for the rule of law. What would it mean publicly to expose torture, to bring it out into the open, to make it emerge from the underground world of state secrets where it is usually practised behind a cloak of denial that hides any trace of it? We live centuries after the end of the age of spectacular and atrocious torments and after the precarious and hard-won abolition of torture. What would it mean in this context to return openly to using torture – however exceptionally – in a democracy? What risks does this entail?

The institutionalization of torture undermines the idea of justice. It makes the state a legal torturer. Torture does not so much push the state into the space where the law no longer reigns – after all, the state, even the democratic state, can legalize its use. But it leads the state to make illegitimate use of the means that citizens have allowed it for the purposes of guaranteeing their own security. Thus the state contravenes the essential purpose of its own coercive power, and it abuses its monopoly of legitimate violence, delegated to it only in order to avoid the eruption of individual violence. This is what Thomas Hobbes teaches. This delegation is temporary, and it is conditional on the respect of the citizenry, which requests the protection of its human, physical and psychological integrity. This respect is also extended to foreigners, non-citizens and to temporary residents who are guests in that country.

If the state carries out torture, it not only abuses its power but also damages the confidence of its own citizens. Rather than being defended, the citizens are instead unexpectedly wounded, attacked in their defenceless vulnerability. The state that touches a citizen's body is already illegitimate – even if that citizen is a prisoner. If it is an agent or a functionary of the state who carries out this violence, then the state can and must intervene to sanction the guilty perpetrator and restore civil order. But who will hand down such sanctions when the state itself has become a legal torturer?

We understand the reasons why the agent or functionary who illegitimately uses violence tends to hide, to operate in secret, to act as if he were acting in his own name and not in the name of the coercive power that he derives from state authority. This allows the state to intervene as a third, mediating body in each bodily clash between its own agent and the violated subject. For in this clash the very space of politics risks being eliminated. Precisely in so far as the violence is being perpetrated against an 'other' who is meant to be inviolable – and this should be the basis of any democracy – torture has the acrid and repugnant smell of a return to a state of nature and the law of the jungle. The institutionalization of torture contradicts the very purpose of the democratic state. Suddenly there is no longer a regulating body; the rule of law is undermined. More than that, in the last analysis the state is cancelling itself out.

Individuals who are legally tortured are 'enemies' rather than citizens; and yet legalized torture expands the terrain of its destructive activity. It involves not only the torturer and the victim, but all members of the community. For everyone then knows that this violence – simultaneously both legal and illegitimate – is being exercised in their name. They can delude themselves that a surgically precise torture, in the context of a state of exception, is not pervasive. But they would soon have to abandon this illusion because, once torture has become a legally recognized institution, it will degenerate into a general policy that corrupts the whole body of society. Democracies, which imagine themselves distinct from totalitarian regimes in this regard, discover that they are not immune either.

17   A shipwreck of human rights?

Is there an absolute ban, or can some exception be made? To those who justify torture without reservation in the name of *raison d'état*, as happens under dictatorial regimes, the only possible alternative is the abolitionist one. This is the position assumed by international bodies and humanitarian organizations from the United Nations to the Red Cross, Amnesty International and Human Rights Watch. Those who purport to take the various forms of a middle position when they call for an exceptional use of torture agreed in law – exceptions that could easily multiply – end up finding themselves on the side of the advocates of torture.

The clash is all the more acute, and all the more urgent, because liberal democracy is not resistant to torture, and can even legalize it without thereby formally losing its own democratic order. To explode a myth: democracy is not of itself humane, respectful or decent. By 'decent' we mean – together with Avishai Margalit (1998) – a society that does not humiliate anyone. It is precisely the link between each individual and the human community – the heart of the democratic project which must be preserved above all else – that may be wounded or broken. And that is what happens with torture, which is extreme violence, the most serious transgression of the principle of respect for humanity. As the era of global terror would suggest, we might make a democratic decision through parliamentary channels or in a referendum to allow exceptional recourse to torture. But then we would need to ask whether we can still speak of a 'democracy' beyond its formal requisites.

What has happened in the United States since 9/11 is not a unique and isolated phenomenon. It concerns all western democracies. One paradoxical case is Italy, which having not recognized torture as a crime, has left room for a practice behind the scenes that deeply corrodes confidence in democracy.

Torture feeds on excess; it is pampered by a lack of a sense of proportion. It thus requires limits. The sentence issued by

Israel's Supreme Court on 6 September 1999 was exemplary in this regard. Unlike the *Kronjuristen* of the US administration, who bowed to executive pressure by justifying torture, the constitutional judges in Israel took a different course that defended the rule of law. The Supreme Court was summoned to examine the legality of four interrogation techniques used by the Shin Bet, the Israeli security services. In particular, these included forced sleep deprivation and the playing of deafeningly loud music (the *shabach* method). While the Supreme Court recognized the threat posed by terrorism, it banned all four of the interrogation techniques concerned, and in general any form of coercion and debasement. It stipulated that the face must never be covered. Most importantly, it declared that all coercive interrogation damages the 'freedom and dignity' of both those subjected to it and those who practise it, raising 'fundamental legal, ethical and political questions' (see Levinson 2004: 165 ff.). That is not to say that the problem has been resolved. The Public Committee Against Torture in Israel has continued to report abuses and maltreatment, and not only against Palestinian detainees.[8] But the constitutional court response was important in setting boundaries to state power, drawing a line beyond which it would become illegitimate.

Moreover, international law is itself explicit in this regard, calling for an absolute ban. The UN Convention's Article 2.2 affirms that 'no exceptional circumstances whatsoever . . . may be invoked as a justification of torture'. Torture humiliates, wounds, degrades – it undermines human dignity. The question of torture is closely bound to the complex topic of human rights. Only on the basis of what are often defined as 'non-negotiable' principles can we reject torture.

The Franco-Argentinian psychoanalyst Miguel Benasayag, arrested and tortured during the Videla military dictatorship, has recounted his own traumatic experience (2005 [1981]). But he has also critically reflected on the connection between torture and human rights. How can we refute those who would seek to legitimize its use as a lesser evil? A 'humanist-philanthropic' response is not enough, for it is too banal and not persuasive enough. Nor can we just invoke the

---

[8] See the site http://stoptorture.org.il/?lang=en

ambiguous 'ideology of human rights', which risks being an inconsistent line of defence, temporarily erected as a sterile rearguard action (1986: 24–9).

Benasayag asks why someone like him, arrested one autumn evening while he walked along the famous Avenida Corrientes in central Buenos Aires, was immediately blind-folded by soldiers or policemen passing themselves off as civilians or para-state bodies. Why, even after this, did his tormentors shrink from being identified as state functionaries, even though they were torturing him in a well-known army barracks? And why, when it was all over, was the humanitar-ian organizations' goal to denounce the role of the Argentin-ian state in this brutal repression, in the ferocious practice of torture? Benasayag's response is that no regime – not even a dictatorship – will ever admit to using torture because this would mean admitting its own illegitimacy. Torture is not just one of many human rights violations, but the final frontier, the violation of the fundamental prohibition represented by the human body as a symbolic limit. In this sense, torture is 'an ancient union that constitutes a psychotic act at the basis of human civilisation' (1986: 67).

While he calls for a deeper reflection – one that phi-losophers have usually abstained from, perhaps precisely because torture is the area of violence that does not allow access to speech – Benasayag scrutinizes the bland appeal to our 'humanity', so vague as to allow it to be emphatically commonplace.

Such an appeal to human rights is unprecedented, not only in respect to torture. Yet the risk is that, despite the suppos-edly universal character of these rights, each person interprets them differently. And conflict often results from this, too. It is as if the human rights code were a sort of artificial lan-guage, the product of an ethics without historical depth that aspires to spread across the surface by promising abstract connections.

Besides, in the wake of the Holocaust, it became dramati-cally clear that those human rights that stop at the borders of the nation-state – thus being more a case of citizens' rights – had failed. What of the refugee? What of the human being deprived of any statehood who ought to be defended and protected precisely on account of this defenceless humanity?

Agamben has picked up on this paradox, first outlined by Arendt, in order to demonstrate how human rights that are considered sacred and inviolable instead prove to be obsolete, leaving 'bare life' exposed to power. What results from this is the 'separation between the humanitarian and the political' that explains the difficulty in which supranational bodies – from the UN to the High Commission for Refugees – and humanitarian organizations find themselves caught. They are forced either to circumscribe their activity within state limits or, worse, to act against their own wishes and replicate the biopolitical paradigm, treating human life in its nakedness (Agamben 2017: 109 ff.).

18   Human dignity in torture

If we look beyond human rights, the core of the problem is the concept of 'human dignity'. This concept enjoys enormous authority at the international level, surrounded by a sacral aura. But what does it mean? There is no conflict in which the different sides do not invoke human dignity. From problems of bioethics or biotechnology to reforms in the welfare state, and from questions of international law to the debate over torture, human dignity is assumed as a norm, indicated as a criterion, asserted as if it were a postulate. Since the end of the Second World War, it has become the unshakable foundation of human rights. Tellingly, this is the very basis of *Grundgesetz* in the German constitution.

Having first appeared within the religious and metaphysical context, only later, in the modern era, has human dignity been carried across to jurisprudence and ethics. Over the last century, it emerged in the international landscape in a first-rank role. In Roman law, *dignitas* indicates the standard incumbent upon public authority. But only in medieval political theology – as Kantorowicz (1997) has shown – was dignity entirely separated from the individual person and carried across to a political or religious post. Hence the motto *dignitas numquam perit*, 'dignity never perishes', meaning the dignity of the post will continue, even if its holder changes or if whoever happens to hold that post is not up to standard. The post and the person are separated from one another.

When dignity enters the moral sphere, it ends up also having the inverse meaning: a person who conducts themselves as if they held office is dignified, even if they do not have such a post. Independent of his social rank, the class to which he belongs or his merits and failings, each human being has a value of his own which demands respect. Human dignity appears simultaneously as both a descriptive and a normative concept: it is the prerogative that is owed to each human being but it entails a duty to be up to this standard, a duty which is entrusted to the community no less than to the individual. Recognition of the other and self-esteem must contribute to the defence of human dignity. Dignity means that persons do not conduct themselves as if they were no one, or as if they were just a thing. We can agree with Karl Kraus in saying that 'Dignity is the conditional form of the human verb' (Kraus 2001: 112).

But we see how slippery this concept remains. Perhaps Ernst Tugendhat is not wholly wrong when he claims that 'there remain only empty words whose meaning cannot be verified' (1995: 145). Yet human dignity is apparent precisely when it is wounded; it displays its full significance in extreme cases of humiliation, offence, debasement and outrage. For this reason alone, it should be maintained as an ethical and political demand.

Torture is the most extreme situation in which human dignity is radically wounded. When the torturer touches his victim, he cancels out his own otherness. Any space between the two disappears. The butcher violates the body, usurps the self and occupies the victim's own world. And this plunges the victim into a dark night of abjection. When dignity collapses and cannot be reclaimed, the vertigo of the inhuman begins.

Among the few philosophers who have reflected on torture, it was Sartre who outlined a phenomenology in which a perverse relationship emerges between torturer and tortured. From his reflection on sadomasochism in his work *Being and Nothingness* to his short text introducing Henri Alleg's pamphlet *La question* – a courageous denunciation of the torture practised by the French in Algeria – Sartre identified in the unique connection between butcher and victim a variant of the dialectical relationship between slave and master, as illustrated by Hegel.

1943, rue Lauriston, Paris and 1958, El Biar, Algiers – little has changed, except that this time it is the French who are degrading others as well as themselves, inflicting violence on those they consider subhuman. This is the same conviction that Sartre expresses in his preface to Frantz Fanon's *Wretched of the Earth* (2011). In this context of colonialism, exploitation and slavery, it is obvious that the French would torture the subhumans, humiliate them, break their pride, prove that they are just animals. This is Alleg's terrible experience: 'They made him a martyr in our name', Sartre comments (Alleg 1958: 10).

In the obscene hive of activity that Alleg describes, the dominant force is a radical hatred, an 'errant and anonymous' hatred which passes from butcher to victim. 'This hatred is torture, erected as a System' (1958: 13). As Sartre had underlined years before, the goal of this system is to 'annihilate the humanity of the next man'. And this is what the interrogation offers: it ensures that with his cries the victim proves and vouches for the fact that he is an animal, in both his own eyes and those of others. 'Mutual killing is the rule; we have always been fighting for collective and particularist interests. But in this strange contest called torture, the stakes seem to be total: the butcher vies with the victim for the title of 'man' itself; and everything takes place as if the two could not both belong to the human species' (1958: 17).

Torture goes far beyond questioning: it is not practised in order to interrogate and extract a confession. Instead, it is the torturers – these sadistic surgeons, these rabid archangels – who want proof of their own total sovereignty. But however shameful and lurid the crime of torture may be, we ought not give in to the derangement of the inhuman and its enchantment. The victim faced with this fierce and grotesque bedlam can oppose his own silence. He can resist. In so doing, he unbinds himself from the butcher's perverse grip and frees himself of an ambiguous passivity. The roles are reversed. This is the supreme irony that the torturer runs into. When the victim resists his suffering and keeps quiet, it is he who ultimately decides the outcome of this abhorrent duel. The victim's resistance strikes fear into the archangel of rage, who must bid farewell to his sovereignty. This was how the seemingly defenceless Alleg could still triumph; this was how the 'humanism of the victims and the colonized had won out' (1958: 20). In this militant vision, the tortured man frees himself and redeems himself; and, fundamentally, he also frees and redeems the torturer. Alleg is the figure of the communist fighter who wins. So in torture there is the possibility of redemption. As in the dialectic of slave and master, here, too, the roles are reversed to the victim's advantage. In Sartre's philosophy, torture takes on a particular value. It becomes the prototype of the human relation in its most violent form, from which it is possible – or rather, necessary – to free ourselves. It is the choice between freedom and nothingness.

We would like to believe in this optimistic vision. But we ought to resist its allure. First of all, torture can never be seen as a duel. Still less can it be seen as a test of wills. The victim cannot defend himself. Rather, he is a defenceless body on which is exercised a boundless rage, the absolute arbitrary power of the butcher. And in this sense, this latter has always already won. The singular case of the martyr who keeps quiet, who puts up a heroic resistance, is not sufficient to cast the light of redemption on torture.

But there is more. If the tormentor is to prove his sovereignty, he has to show that the torture victim does not belong to the same 'human species', in the sense that Antelme meant it (1947). That is, it is necessary to strip him of any dignity and keep him in that limbo between life and death as indicated by Kant. The torturer does not kill him. He makes him live and lets him die, as in the famous formula with which Foucault summarized modern biopolitics (2003: 241). It is there, in the gloomy and abject interregnum of torture, that by using all manner of methods he pushes him towards the non-human, breaking the tortured man's link with humanity. This is a decisive threshold. Once it has been crossed, the path of return and the path of redemption do not coincide. It is possible to get out of the abyss of the inhuman, for the tortured man no less than for the torturer, who has also degraded himself in his plunge into the abyss, but not without leaving lasting damage. The effects of torture cannot be rubbed away. Dignity no longer seems recoverable.

2

Phenomenology of Torture

[T]he very phenomenon of suffering in its uselessness is, in principle, the pain of the other. For an ethical sensibility, confirming, in the inhumanity of our time, its opposition to this inhumanity, the justification of the neighbour's pain is certainly the source of all immorality.

Emmanuel Levinas, *Entre Nous: Thinking-of-the-Other*

1 Defining torture: etymological notes

What is torture? If we want to answer this question, then first of all we have to look back to its etymology. The word 'torture' derives from the Latin verb *torquere* (to twist, to wring, to wind) – from which derive the French verb *tordre*, the Italian *torcere* and English verbs like 'contort' and 'distort'. Its root is *terk- or *trek-, which suggests a pulling motion. For instance, we can twist a branch, a shoot or a vine, pull and bend it or flatten it out by stretching it. And we do the same to the parts of the human body. When we get a sprained ankle, we contort the bone back into shape. The etymology is transparent: since its very origins, torture has been connected to the stretching of the body. However, here the stretches that we perform for therapeutic purposes pass from a medical vocabulary to a legal one. In this latter context, torture designates that twisting and pulling of members that ought to help repair some injustice, some offence, some outrage or – as we say with deference to the verb *torquere* – a 'tort'.

The passage from medical torsion to judicial torture is not, then, so much a metaphor: in each case, we contort the parts of the body in order to put things back in place, to correct and to make amends. Torture, then, is therapeutic for the community. Just as we bend a piece of wood, whose shape has somehow been distorted, we contort the body of the suspected criminal in order to straighten it out. This, then, is also the way to restore equilibrium in the community. Justice inscribes itself on the body. It is not a doctor who does this, but rather his sinister alter ego, the torturer. The torturer distorts and contorts in order to get a confession; but the use of this violence is itself punishment for the crime. It smashes and crushes the body; it grinds it into dust, as if it were a piece of wood. To this end, it makes use of the *tormentum*, the instrument of torture. There is no limit to the imagination, no limit to the equipment at the butcher's disposal to provide punishment, torment and torture. And as Lafaye tells us, torment, which like 'torture' derives from *torqueo*, is no less etymologically telling:

> [The name torment] must originally have referred above all to those instruments that caused the tightening of the muscles and the leaking-out of utterances, with the aid of ropes which were gradually pulled more tense: thus in particular the rack (*equuleus*), the apparatus called the *fiduculae* and the wheel (*rota*). With time, however, *tormentum* came to acquire a more general meaning. (1916: 362)

From cause to effect: 'torment' indicates not only, and not so much, the action that causes pain but the pain itself. While it does not lose its concrete value, its carnal foundation, its meaning expands to become synonymous with distress and trouble. The same is true of 'torture': as it expands its semantic field, it can designate an act of cruelty, or metaphorically come to signify some physical or psychological suffering. Or it can refer, in hyperbolic terms, to some difficulty or anxiety.

We might say that all this is nothing special. As we know, metaphors open up new areas of understanding as they transpose from the concrete onto the more abstract. Yet torture not only expands its realm of meaning, almost as far as to dilute and dissolve its first, dark meaning, but it also tries to hide itself away. The ancient Roman talk of the *quaestio* was but the first of a long series of euphemisms. Here, torture takes up residence in the landscape of the law, in that place where the accused is subjected to questioning. It pursues legality through its ancient and never decisively broken alliance with interrogation. Here, torture is 'questioning' – another way of saying interrogation. Yet this fiction does not entirely succeed. For the arena of law does not coincide with the torture cell, nor the practice of questioning with the inquisition. If interrogation is itself to be legal, then it must exclude torture from the landscape of the law.

How, then, should we define torture? This is significant, given that the definition of torture is itself an arena for deciding whether we should incriminate torture or else liberalize it by resorting to some other name, whether we should declare it a crime or make it legal. The boundaries of the dictionary definition here become the boundaries of the law. The famous Torture Memo is no isolated case. Elsewhere, too, the attempt is made to manipulate the boundaries: its scope is restricted so that waterboarding or forced sleep deprivation are not considered torture, or so that particular characteristics can be added on. These more or less awkward attempts to advance the pretence that 'coercive interrogation' is not torture are probably destined to repeat themselves. Their credibility and effectiveness depend on the defences that public opinion sets up against them. But they will not be stopped by any mere definition of the concept. Contrary to what we might imagine, such a definition can itself become the pretext for legalistic quibbling and dangerous sophistry. Even the way in which the UN expressed itself in the Convention against Torture is problematic (see Brecher 2007: 5). Any term is open to misunderstanding or more or less deliberate misinterpretation. Moreover, the definitions that have thus far been provided follow the line of causation, whereas it would be appropriate to look rather more at the effects, as Rejali (2007: 562) has suggested. Defining a concept is, however, a philosophical difficulty. We are compelled to identify what is different about it in order to glean some essence which is wholly phantom and yet supposed to be more real than reality itself. Nietzsche used the example of the leaf, observing that 'Just as no leaf is ever exactly the same as any other, certainly the concept "leaf" is formed by arbitrarily dropping those individual differences, by forgetting the distinguishing factors' (1989: 249). Definition is a useless metaphysical abstraction. As Wittgenstein made clear, 'We don't believe that only someone who can provide a definition of the concept "game" really understands a game' (2013: 903). So we should give up on trying to define some concept of torture, which would invariably leave out some method and not take into account the full complexity of this practice as it transforms across history. Torture's various modalities are linked by family resemblances that allow us in each case to agree when the word should be used and enable us to draw up a grammar of torture.

It is, then, more useful to describe the phenomenon than to define it. Philosophers from Aristotle to Seneca and from Augustine to Thomas of Aquinas, often overlooking torture's ethical aspect, have interrogated its effectiveness and the truth of the confession thus extorted (see Foucault 2013: 197). But what is lacking is a phenomenology of torture. This has only been outlined in broad brush strokes.

2   'Whoever has succumbed to torture can no longer feel at home in the world' (Améry)

As he seeks out his origins, Jacques Austerlitz, protagonist of Winfried Georg Sebald's great novel, goes to Belgium. There, among other things, he visits the Breendonk fortress, between Antwerp and Brussels. During the Nazi occupation, the Germans had designated it an *Auffanglager* – internment camp – before it became the Museum of the Belgian Resistance from 1947 onwards. Austerlitz describes it in a wealth of detail, giving us a mental map of the fortress, and tells of the moment that he entered the *Folterkammer*, the underground bunker where the SS tortured its victims. He then adds:

it was only a few years later that I read Jean Améry's description of the dreadful physical closeness between torturers and their victims, and of the tortures he himself suffered in Breendonk when he was hoisted aloft by his hands, tied behind his back, so that with a crack and a splintering sound which, as he says, he had not yet forgotten when he came to write his account, his arms dislocated from the sockets in his shoulder joints, and he was left dangling as they were wrenched up behind him and twisted together above his head. (Sebald 2013: 29)

Améry's essay, which appears in the collection *Jenseits von Schuld und Sühne*, is a description, the author himself tells us, of his *Opfer-Existenz*, his 'existence as a victim'. It has become one of the reference works on torture and is certainly among the most widely cited (see Perret 2013). Its capacity for introspection, the depth of Améry's reflection and the rawness of the language penetrating the folds of pain, make this work an extraordinary testimony, as well as a milestone in the phenomenology of torture.

Améry was arrested while he was distributing leaflets as part of a small Belgian Resistance group. In the Gestapo HQ, they subjected him to interrogation. 'Your accomplices?', they barked. Améry did not speak. For he knew only their *noms de guerre*. This was a widespread means by which a group prevented any individual member from giving up the names of the others. He was then taken to Breendonk and left in the hands of the SS. The date that marked the caesura in his life was 23 July 1943, when they began to torture him.

With the first blow, his trust in the world was broken forever. '[T]he certainty that by reason of written or unwritten social contracts the other person will spare me – more precisely stated, that he will respect my physical, and with it also my metaphysical, being' collapsed (Améry 1980: 28). Torture violates the boundaries of the body, which are the boundaries of the ego. The other imposes his own corporeity. It is 'like a rape', Améry writes. In describing this abuse perpetrated against the flesh, he employs the unusual German term *Verfleischlichung*: the complete reduction of the human being to flesh. And when there is nothing else but flesh, through the pain '[i]n self-negation, his flesh becomes a total reality' (1980: 33). *Verfleischlichung* is not only the expulsion of the spirit, but also a modality of death (see Weber 2012: 88–9). This body, of which pain has now taken possession, is a body that is already dying. Torture 'allows us to experience [death] personally' (Améry 1980: 34).

The tortured person is brought near to death, from which point he can, if necessary, be pushed over the edge, into Nothingness. Torture is *Vernichtung*, annihilation. There is no place either for autonomy or resistance (see Kramer 2004: 450). Améry belies the anti-fascist taboo of the resistance militant who never betrays his comrades: 'I talked. I accused myself of invented absurd political crimes' (1980: 36). He implicitly sets himself apart from Sartre, who was in fact his point of reference, as his 1971 essay *Unmeisterliche Wanderjahre* demonstrates. He puts into doubt the philosophy of resistance. He casts himself as the anti-hero, a mirror-image opposed to Henri Alleg, who instead stated that: 'I was impassioned by the battle I had engaged without giving in, by the thought that I was heading toward death as I had always hoped, faithful to my ideal, to my comrades in struggle' (1958: 73). For Améry, the martyrdom of torture provided no release or redemption. Defenceless and helpless, the tortured man is abandoned to himself. It is as if the community to which he belonged – even his political community – has dissolved. Thus 'torture is the most horrible event a human being can retain within himself' (Améry 1980: 22).

Is it possible to describe it, then? Améry seems wedded to the traditional thesis according to which pain, and even more so the pain inflicted by torture, is impossible to communicate; it is so extreme that it eludes mere words. Yet at the same time, he is writing in order to speak not of the *wie*, the 'how', but of the *was*, the 'what'. Conscious of the unbridgeable gap between language and his own physical sensations, he aims at a *sachliche Beschreibung*, a description that relates in detail how things happened. And the torture scene is the dramatic epicentre of the whole essay:

> In the bunker there hung from the vaulted ceiling a chain that above ran into a roll. At its bottom end it bore a heavy, broadly curved iron hook. I was led to the instrument. The hook gripped into the shackle that held my hands together behind my back. Then I was raised with the chain until I hung

about a meter over the floor. In such a position, or rather, when hanging this way, with your hands behind your back, for a short time you can hold at a half-oblique through muscular force. During these few minutes, when you are already expending your utmost strength, when sweat has already appeared on your forehead and lips, and you are breathing in gasps, you will not answer any questions. Accomplices? Addresses? Meeting places? You hardly hear it. All your life is gathered in a single, limited area of the body, the shoulder joints, and it does not react; for it exhausts itself completely in the expenditure of energy. But this cannot last long, even with people who have a strong physical constitution. As for me, I had to give up rather quickly. And now there was a crackling and splintering in my shoulders that my body has not forgotten until this hour. The balls sprang from their sockets. My own body weight caused luxation; I fell into a void and now hung by my dislocated arms, which had been torn high from behind and were now twisted over my head. Torture, from the Latin *torquere*, to twist. What visual instruction in etymology! (Améry 1980: 32)

In this narrative drama, neither sensations nor feeling filter through. The tortured man's 'scream of pain and death' (1980: 35) does burst, uncontrollable, into the text. But no concession is made to aesthetic pathos. For this reason, elsewhere, in his film critiques, Améry lauds Costas-Gravas's film *L'Aveu*, in which 'the torture scenes are shot in their stark facticity' (1994: 87).

Torture has a *character indelebilis*. Even once any trace of the torture has disappeared, the tortured man remains . . . tortured. Torture is an indelibly printed mark. From that extreme limit, there is no return. That owes to the *Fremdheit*, the estrangement, which no words can ever heal. The victim realizes, stunned – feeling it on his own skin – that the other can set himself up as 'absolute sovereign'. The sovereignty of the persecutor, the *Folterknecht* – literally, torture's servant – is but the 'unlimited triumph' of the survivor. And in one of the most renowned passages of the essay, summing up his reflection, Améry concludes:

Whoever has succumbed to torture can no longer feel at home in the world. The shame of destruction cannot be erased. Trust in the world, which already collapsed in part at the first blow, but in the end, under torture, fully, will not be regained. That one's fellow man was experienced as the antiman remains in the tortured person as accumulated horror. It blocks the view into a world in which the principle of hope rules. (Améry 1980: 40)

3 Torture, genocide, Holocaust

Even if historically speaking the unconditional ban on torture was an immediate consequence of the reaction against the horrors of Auschwitz, in no sense can torture be considered an essential characteristic of the Holocaust. Even though in its latest forms torture does make up part of biopolitics, on closer inspection it is not an integral part of either genocide or extermination. To extend the terminology of the concentration camp to the phenomenon of torture – when, for example, we think that we can recognize the figure of the tortured man also in the *Muselmann* – is unjustified and misleading. This risks neglecting the differences and above all overlooking the complex particularities of torture. Such reductionism – which is, alas, very frequent – risks sowing confusion rather than shedding light.

Améry himself contributed to this confusion, when he reaffirmed in his essay that 'torture was the essence of National Socialism' (1980: 30). And moreover that 'Torture was no invention of National Socialism. But it was its apotheosis' (ibid.). Without mentioning him directly, Améry cites the words of the writer Rudolf G. Binding, who had himself rallied to Nazism: 'We Germans are heroic in bearing the suffering of others' (Binding 1933). Améry is making polemical reference to heroism misunderstood as a self-education in cruelty – a theme that he had already addressed in his 1945 essay *Zur Psychologie des deutschen Volkes* (Améry 2002: 500–34).

Given that Améry was later deported to Auschwitz, the experience of torture seems to meld with the experience of the camps. The boundaries are blurred. It is thus no surprise that some interpreters see the genocide as an intensification of torture, or better, a large-scale exercise in torture (see Andersch 1977: 22). In order to authenticate their interpretation, they need only refer to Améry, who besides being the author also has the authority of a survivor and a witness. This should give us cause, among other things, to reflect on the value of testimony. Precious as it is as an irreplaceable source, nonetheless it cannot be accepted as an indisputable historical judgement.

In the Breendonk fortress, torture was inflicted on the partisan, a member of the political resistance who had counterfeit ID documents on him at the time of his arrest. Appalling as it was, this torture scenario had in fact already been seen elsewhere, for example in the prisons of the Guardia Nacional Republicana in Spain. Torture here has two characteristics: it is the violent expression of a fascist regime that practises terror; and it strikes at the individual, humiliated and tormented because he is part of the Resistance. Once he was identified, Améry – as he himself recounts – received the 'death sentence' summarized in the destination Auschwitz. This was the context in which Améry experienced the inevitability that corresponded to his Jewishness. He was deported to Auschwitz not because of a choice he had made and not because of his actions, but rather because of his very being; because he was Jewish. This must have been all the more bitter and incomprehensible to him, given that he had such a distant and negative relationship with his Jewishness. Nonetheless, it was clear to him that, as a Jew, he was likely to die. But even when he narrates his internment, he describes Auschwitz as a concentration camp and not as an extermination camp. Yet, Auschwitz was both. But Améry is silent on the gas chambers, the distinctive site of the Holocaust.

In the case of mass extermination, the individual does not count. She, like others, indeed together with others, enters into chambers that are disguised as showers. Here, she, like the hundreds and thousands of others, within ten minutes or so will die an anonymous death, succumbing to the jets of prussic acid. Everything takes place quickly, efficiently, as if on a production line. No face-to-face confrontation between executioner and victim is called for here. With extermination, there is no time for a relation like the one that is established in torture. Indeed, there is no time for torture. The victim is reduced not to a tormented piece of flesh but to a heap of ashes.

With regard to genocide, we can say that when the aim is to deport and kill entire peoples by all and any means, and when the goal is the elimination of millions, then the use of torture becomes superfluous. What does endure is a mutually supportive contiguity, a well-balanced connivance between the various forms of violence.

That is not to say that torture was not practised in Nazi Germany. The Gestapo's methods, starting with the infamous 'third degree', have entered the history books (see Delarue 2011). The guilty verdict issued by the Nuremburg tribunal made explicit reference to this, albeit in just a few lines. The collaboration of doctor with the Nazis, recounted in great detail by Robert Jay Lifton, occupies an entire chapter, although Lifton uses the term 'torture' only twice (2000: 200, 209). For a profession that abandoned the idea of care in order to sign up to the biopolitical project of eugenics, the experiments conducted within the camps – often directed by universities and scientific institutions – cannot simply be considered as torture.

4   Killing and torturing

There is evidence of torture being practised ever since Antiquity. Over time it has changed and been honed, as the human species has established itself. If we reflect on the crude 'beastliness' of the torturer, we may be surprised to learn that beasts do not torture. We only find some elements of the practice in primates. Deer, dogs, wild animals and pets do not torture. Yet they do kill, driven by animal instinct. Only human beings have developed the inhuman ability to torture. Only they have taken to extremes the consciousness of others' consciousness, the capacity to imagine what the other is imagining, of fearing what the other fears, of experiencing what the other experiences, and inflicted suffering on others' skins in the most incisive possible way, through this paroxysmal and inverted empathy.

What is the difference between killing and torturing? This philosophical question is in many ways decisive, not least because of its political and legal repercussions. Indeed, we often confuse torture with execution, assimilating it to capital punishment, or worse, read the destruction caused by this torment as if it were annihilation, and thus end up immediately situating torture within a context of genocide or extermination. A public debate has been able to develop in the United States – and indeed, for many involved, the debate is aimed at legalizing the practice – because many states permit the death penalty. If they can execute the guilty man with a lethal injection, they do not see why they should not torture him. Fundamentally, torture is seen as inflicting a lesser punishment than death and, unlike an execution, the pain can be relieved. The most over-inflated argument in this sense comes from the German political scientist Uwe Steinhoff. Active in the English-speaking world, Steinhoff is among the most fervent apologists for torture. In his recent work *On the Ethics of Torture*, Steinhoff locates torture among the tools of self-defence, and justifies its use by comparing it to killing (2013: 18 ff.). And yet in a previous article discussing the use of torture, even when the life of only one person is at stake – as practised by Dirty Harry, the policeman played by Clint Eastwood in the eponymous film – Steinhoff writes:

What is so bad about torturing people, anyway? People also kill people. Soldiers kill people, policemen kill people, doctors kill people, executioners kill people and ordinary people kill people. Some of these killings are justified. So why shouldn't it be justified in some cases to torture people? After all, being killed seems to be worse than being tortured. Even most of the tortured people seem to see it this way; otherwise they would kill themselves in order to escape further torture (yes, some do, but they are only a few). So, if killing is sometimes justified, torture too must sometimes be justified. (2008: 97)

This is the result to which the equation between torture and killing might lead. For that matter, this confirms that the exception – the exception of the ticking time bomb – not only easily becomes a rule but also opens the way for what philosophers call the slippery slope fallacy, in this case meaning that torture could be admissible in all circumstances and even as a precautionary measure. The slope that Steinhoff's 'morality' is sliding down is that which calls itself self-defence. If it is deemed legitimate to kill in self-defence, as happens not only in war but also in a lot of other situations, then it should also be legal to torture, especially given that the resulting harm is less, and those subjected to it remain alive.

But in whatever context we look at it, torture is always offensive conduct. It must never be dressed up as self-defence, still less as legitimate self-defence. We need only think of the paradigmatic scenario, i.e. when in a state of war a soldier who is called up to fight on the front may perhaps end up killing an enemy soldier. But pain and suffering affect both of them because the relationship between them is substantially symmetrical. This notwithstanding, killing – even in war – is not in any sense natural or obvious. Evidencing this are the Great War novels, from Tolstoy's *War and Peace* to Erich Maria Remarque's *All Quiet on the Western Front*. What does a soldier experience when he kills another soldier? What about when he does it up close, for instance in the intimate brutality of a stabbing? There is a good reason why weapons have transformed over the centuries, especially in recent, hi-tech decades, with a focus on long-range ballistics that have the potential for a more sanitized and anonymous elimination of the 'enemy', a category that often ends up encompassing even defenceless civilians. The colossal achievements of the mathematics of death only appear to make killing a simpler task. The manual *On Killing: The Psychological Cost of Learning to Kill in War and Society* has become compulsory reading for the FBI, the Marines and many corps of the US Army. Even before he evaluates all the burdensome consequences for the soldier's life *after* war, author Dave Grossman (2009) examines the difficulties that impede the act of killing itself. He asks, 'Why does the soldier not kill?' The most difficult of obstacles is a face-to-face meeting: for the soldier can make out his own eyes in the eyes of the other; in the other's features, in his expression, however hostile, he sees the – however weakened – human bond that still joins them together. This must present even more of an obstacle when he is shooting not in self-defence but at a soldier who has already surrendered. In any context, attacking, wounding or striking someone unable to react appears not only unfair, but morally repugnant.

This asymmetry is a prominent characteristic of torture, in which the victim is unarmed and wholly defenceless in the hands of his persecutor (see Sussman 2005). But there is more: torture is not the outcome of some more or less impromptu action. In this sense, it is distinct from spontaneous forms of violence, for example the act – even a cruel one – that is committed by someone in thrall to anger or some other emotion who acts on impulse. Torture is systematic, organized, methodical violence – all the more violent because it does not erupt but remains under control. With firm will and libidinous tenacity, it turns upon the victim.

Reducing the other to naked impotence gives a sense of unlimited power. This happens a lot more in the context of torture than in the context of killing, for once the other person is dead, he or she becomes a body unable to put up further resistance. The persecutor's drunken exuberance can no longer let rip on the dead person, precisely because the latter is lifeless, just as killing a woman is not the same thing as raping her in front of her husband or having her raped by brothers and sons. Breaking human laws produces a feeling of omnipotence, as if becoming a demi-god; it instills a euphoric sense of absolute sovereignty.

5   Between biopower and sovereign power

Torture is the opposite of creation. That does not mean that it is annihilation; rather, it is the experience of one's own destruction, even while one is still alive. The torturer carefully avoids the torments going too far, working to ensure that the victim's death is kept at bay. For if the victim were to die, the instrument of the torturer's power would disappear. The destruction of the victim is the triumph of the torturer: and this triumph can only be celebrated during the interregnum between life and death.

That is why the tortured person's last gesture may well be to choose death in order to escape the butcher. There are many examples of this. At Guantánamo Bay, there have been repeated hunger strikes. Between January and June 2005, it seems that between 130 and 200 prisoners of around 500 held there at the time refused to eat. According to the *New York Times*'s reconstruction of these hunger strikes, at least twelve of the prisoners were subjected to force-feeding

(Golden 2007). Other sources say that the number was far higher. We can suppose that these strikes recurred repeatedly. Back in June 2009, the Yemeni prisoner Mohammad Ahmed Abdullah Saleh al Hanashi died 'by suicide'. He was detained in the camp for seven years and had been subjected to force-feeding through the nose (Glaberson and Williams 2009).

The prisoner is tortured through waterboarding, forced sleep deprivation, exposure to extreme temperatures, electric shocks, intimidation with dogs, and sexual abuse and humiliation. But alongside this, force-feeding is used to prevent him dying. Is this a contradiction? It is rather more the simultaneous exercise of two distinct logics of power which here coincide: namely, sovereign power and biopower. Written on the detainee's body is the power that consists of what Foucault called 'to make live and to let die'. But if the detainee were to die, this power would reach its limit, for this would mean that he could no longer either be killed or allowed to die. Useful for this power's purposes is the collaboration of medical professionals. They are called upon to monitor the victim's health and to advise on how to prevent his death. Here we have the concentrated focus of a perverse biopower that exercises control over a person's life.

At Guantánamo Bay, torture proved to be the establishment of sovereign power, implemented by means of bio-political techniques. This distinguishes it from torture in the modern era, which does not go so far as clinically calculating the breaking point in order to avoid a detainee's death, nor carries out a paroxysm of force-feeding. But it also distinguishes it from the sovereign power that decides who should live and who should die – this being a decisive component of those thanato-political regimes that seek to protect the body of the nation. In the contemporary form of torture that has been practised at Guantánamo for some years now – and which will presumably not come to an end when Guantánamo closes – biopower does not see its goal as the death of the 'undesirables'. Bodies may be tortured, but they are not killed nor allowed to die. Rather, through an unprecedented synergy, biopower imposes a limit on sovereign power, so that its power over the victim may continue to be exercised.

6   Anatomy of the butcher

The figure of the butcher (*carnefice*) is etymologically connected with flesh (*carne*). The term *carne-fice*, in Latin *carnifex*, consists of *caro*, *carnis*, flesh, and *facere*, to do/make. The material to which the butcher applies his techniques is the flesh of others. In his testimony Améry emphasizes the theme of flesh, the *Fleisch* and *Verfleischlichung* – becoming-flesh – of the tortured person. The butcher's power lies precisely in his reducing a human being to mere flesh while he is still alive. But what does 'flesh' mean? This is a limit-concept that has remained on the edges of philosophy, which has preferred to pass over it in silence. But Maurice Merleau-Ponty did elaborate upon this theme. He spoke of what 'we have previously called flesh', noting that 'one knows there is no name in traditional philosophy to designate it' (1968: 139). Subsequently, the theme has been ignored or treated with diffidence in philosophical debate (see Carbone and Levin 2003). Roberto Esposito notes as much in his work *Bíos*, in which he writes: 'No philosophy has been able to reach that undifferentiated layer (for this very reason exposed to difference) in which the very notion of the body, anything but closed, is now turned to the outside in an irreducible heterogeneity' (2008: 159, translation altered).

Flesh is not the same as the body: it is that part, that membrane, which marks the body's limits. That is as true of the individual body as of the political body. Not by chance, Esposito observes, 'This notion of a material-like, organic and what Merleau-Ponty would have called a "savage" flesh has never had a political configuration.' And, he adds, 'flesh has always belonged to the modality of the impolitical; what political form could it take?' (2008: 164, 166; translation altered).

Seeking to shed light on the theme of flesh outside the body, he refers to Francis Bacon's painting, itself a response to Nazi biopolitical practice. In the imagery of the killing floor and the butchered, deformed, torn flesh, it is only with great disgust that we still recognize the human profile.

But this flesh, almost inorganic matter, that emerges from the body, a bleeding shredded mass, is the same flesh on which the butcher works. This is tortured flesh. Perhaps for this reason, torture has remained at the margins of philosophical discourse. And it is the flesh that is expelled from the political body, as the tortured person's body is reduced to nothing more than flesh. This is doubtless a further meaning of the term *Verfleischlichung* coined by Améry, and indeed a decisively important one. The butcher's task now appears clearer, but also more complex. We understand – as the Uruguayan psychoanalysts Viñar and Viñar have underlined – that 'the tortured person appears as the incarnated witness of a scourge that concerns humanity as a whole' (1989: 163).

The butcher's work goes beyond physical destruction. In his hands, the victim is transformed into a dying being, lacerated flesh, the *disjecta membra* of a body that is no longer a body, quasi-inorganic matter that nonetheless continues to live. This is, therefore, an interminable agony, an execution that is repeatedly suspended and resumed. The tortured person experiences himself, alive, as a piece of flesh outside of his body, whose strangeness is irredeemable, and to which he even feels hostile. For the victim's body is the weapon used against him.

The butcher operates according to the cold mechanics of cause and effect. He calculates and measures, proceeding with established expertise, detached impassiveness and diligent self-sacrifice. And while he works on the bound and immobile naked body, he has the satisfaction of experiencing his power, this expansion of himself proportional to the contraction of the victim's body. The apotheosis comes when there is nothing left but flesh.

7 Sade, the negation of the other, and the language of violence

What does the butcher's *modus operandi* have to do with sadism? Many dismiss any such link, because they take sadism to mean a sexual pathology, indeed one that can offer a rather easier alibi. Nonetheless, it is legitimate, or rather appropriate, to speak of sadism in a more properly philosophical register, all the more so, given that Sade was perhaps the first biopolitical thinker of modernity, the thinker who identified and proclaimed the political meaning of sexuality. Nor is it difficult to grasp the bond that links the sadist to the sovereign. There are no few affinities between the rigid rules that apply in the inaccessible Château de Silling, described in the famous novel *The 120 Days of Sodom*, and those that order life in an internment camp.

Even when Améry polemically emphasizes the need for a 'non-banal understanding of evil', he recognizes the stamp of sadism in his tormentors – a stamp to which he traces all Nazism. The sadist wants to cancel out this world, destroying his own kind and reducing it to flesh. Thus he can impose his own total sovereignty. This is sadism as the philosophy and politics of negation.

Sartre delved into the political-existential aspect of sadism. In *Being and Nothingness*, he saw its genesis in the break in reciprocity when the other is no longer anything but flesh to be made one's own: 'Sadism is passion, barrenness, and tenacity' (1984: 517). His cool passion is no oxymoron: the sadist is dogged in his commitment to enslave the other, but only in an instrumental sense and only when the other is 'incarnated' through violence. In this immediate appropriation, the sadist enjoys the use of his own body a free and appropriative power employed as a means of inflicting pain on the flesh of the other. This is an obscene relation. If the other's freedom lies in his partial inaccessibility – in flesh, both veiled and revealed – the sadist's craving for obscenity makes the flesh appear, forcibly denuded and manhandled. Nonetheless, it would be a mistake to think that the sadist wants only the other to be made flesh. Upon closer inspection, we see he has a further purpose: he wants to make the other swallow his freedom, imprisoned in his flesh. And he insists on proof that this enslavement has indeed come about: he thus humiliates, threatens and tortures him. Here, in torture, we should grasp that taste for domination that emerges with sadism, born of his 'disturbance' 'faced with the other' (1984: 518). The peak of the butcher's pleasure is the moment in which the victim reneges on himself; for the apostasy is now a free one. When the pain becomes unbearable, the victim capitulates and humiliates himself; in so doing, he freely gives confirmation that his own freedom has been reduced to tortured flesh. Remorse and shame will bring him no peace. Even if he does manage to survive, he will not be able to forget that palpitating, obscene flesh, the image of his shattered freedom.

But a defeat is also lying in store for the sadist, owing not only to the mere instrumental use of his own body. Nor is it only because he no longer knows what to do with the carnality that lies in front of him, which he has used but can no longer appropriate, precisely because it is material flesh. The defeat lies in the other's gaze. When his victim looks at him, the sadist discovers that the other's freedom, which he truly wanted to appropriate for himself, inevitably eludes him, even when the other has been entirely humiliated and enslaved. Sadism runs aground in the face of the other's gaze.

However, it runs aground only after it has already brought destruction. Klossowski (1991) has identified in Sade's destructive impulse the traces of a Manichean gnosis that particularly took form in Marcion. Originally, there was a purity, which has now been lost for ever. It is assumed that the present time, in which it is no longer possible to find redemption, will play out as a progressive degeneration. This is, therefore, the opposite of the idea of progress that asserted itself in Enlightenment thinking in these same years. Sade would, then, be a modern gnostic heresiarch: if the creation is a cursed Fall, the human body is nothing but a prison.

From Barthes to Deleuze – and this latter considered Sade's work not pornographic, but rather pornological – many writers have challenged the vision of sadism as pathology. But it was particularly Georges Bataille who offered an original interpretation of sadism, in part adopted also by Améry.

Sade's system decrees the birth of the full individual who aspires to absolute sovereignty, under the banner of an immense negation – above all meaning the negation of others. 'The greatest pain for others always counts for less than my own pleasure' – that was how Maurice Blanchot summarized Sade's morality (1949: 220). It does not matter if it takes a shocking accumulation of crimes in order to achieve some pleasure for oneself. This conduct derives from recognition of the solitude to which each of us is condemned. Why, then, should we not prefer what makes us happy, anywhere at any time? Bataille takes this as a cue to trace a reversal that emerges within absolute sovereignty. If at the beginning the negation of others is an affirmation of the self, very soon the limits of this self-assertion come to light. Sovereignty proves illusory as soon as the sovereign, in his unlimited power, is no longer free to disregard the law. Transgression disappears, and with it any sensual pleasure. The negation of others thus turns inside out, becoming a negation of the self. And it is then, with this recoil, that in cruel disillusionment – which has already become cruelty – there remains nothing but crime and the aberration of continuing in crime.

Perhaps sadism is an 'excrescence' that each person bears within themselves – a sovereign and irreducible part of them, which evades their own consciousness. Bataille suggests that this would imply that humanity entails some excess that drives it to destruction (1986). Sadism would, then, be another way of referring to that destructive potential which lurks within all existence – the impulse not to allow one's neighbour to exist, hence the totalitarian strain identified by Améry, the cancelling out of any relationship with the other.

Yet for Bataille what distinguishes Sade is the paradox of his language. His descriptions of shocking scenes of torture, of bloodied cadavers, of women whose throats have been cut, do not correspond to the hypocritical language of the butcher. In the latter's case, violence is not mentioned, or is only mentioned so that it might be justified. Yet the violent man also proves deceptive. The legally authorized butcher resorts to the language of power, the idiom of state bureaucracy. When Sade's characters openly assert the sovereign value of crimes, of torments, of excesses, they transgress the silence in which violence always wishes to conceal itself. Also because of the total negation which it entails, violence is mute. Sade stands opposed to the butcher because he himself reports the crime, articulating violence and converting it into a reflection on violence.

8   From Torquemada to Scilingo: four portraits

Perhaps no figure is as sinister and disturbing, as enigmatic and perverse, as the torturer. Whether assuming the haughty aspect of the inquisitor or hiding behind the executioner's cruel mask, over time the torturer has surrounded himself with the fabulous aura of myth. He has thus occupied a front-rank role in the shared imaginary, which literature has itself fed. We need only think of Dostoyevsky's Grand Inquisitor (1969 [1880]). This has helped to push him back into an unknown and reassuring remoteness. It is as if the torturer's monstrous, diabolical traits were not even human.

But who really is the torturer? How has this figure appeared across the course of history? Can we identify characteristics that continually repeat themselves, whatever the other differences? In order to respond to this question, it is worth providing broad brush-stroke portraits of four figures in particular. The first and the historically most distant – but for this no less famous, or infamous – is Tomás de Torquemada. Others, closer to our own time but perhaps less well known, are the French general Paul Aussaresses, Kaing Guek Eav, known as Duch, a leader of the Khmer Rouge; and lastly, the Argentine Adolfo Scilingo. As in the case of the distinction we made between torture and extermination, when we look at torturers we should remove any grounds for confusion. The issue is not only the quantity, the gigantic number of victims eliminated in the production lines that worked night and day in the workshops of Hitlerism. The decisive point is the face-to-face encounter. The Nazis well knew this. That is why they barricaded themselves behind their desks. It is well known that Adolf Eichmann never tortured or killed anyone personally. But that does not in any way reduce his boundless, epochal guilt. The torturer has assumed different roles in the hierarchy, from the simple jailer to the commandant of an internment camp. But above all he is the figure who has to look the victim in the eye as he inflicts violence upon them. That is the case even where he has restricted himself to ordering violence. To torture is not to kill – the industrialization of death has no equivalent in the industrialization of torture. This is why torture is a contemplated, distilled violence that requires a face-to-face encounter, no less than a full-contact meeting between bodies.

Perhaps not everyone knows that in the trappings of a Dominican friar – the confessor of Isabelle of Castile and Ferdinand the Catholic, and later the first great inquisitor of Castile and Aragon – there hid the descendant of a family of *conversos*, i.e. Jews who had converted to Christianity, usually when forced to but sometimes of their own free will. Only in 1482, having already reached 61 years of age, did Torquemada make his entrance onto the stage of history. Within little more than a year, when called on to organize the general tribunal of the Inquisition in Seville, until his death in 1498, he would remain the inquisitor-general. In this post he was the only public official whose authority – far beyond that of the Reyes Católicos – was recognized across all of New Spain, where he became a symbol. His name is still linked today to an unspecified number of victims, jailed, humiliated, tortured and burned at the stake. His legacy, however, resides in the architecture of the Inquisition and his secret methods. Heralding a modern bureaucracy, Torquemada created a system that was based on spying and a powerful judicial apparatus. This system functioned through myriad channels, thanks to the climate of suspicion, fear and insecurity. Thus in the Inquisition we can already discern an embryonic thought police. The legalistic obsession and meticulous methods of Torquemada – who was also author of the Compilación de las instrucciones del Oficio de la Santa Inquisición – explain the imposing collection of records from the Inquisition which remain today, some of which are yet to be deciphered. Yirmiyahu Yovel, who sees in the Spanish Inquisition the first form of 'modern dictatorship', has compared these records to those built up by Stalin's bureaucracy, the Stasi, i.e. the East German secret police (see Yovel 2009: 162).

More impenetrable is Torquemada's own personality. His actions were dictated by faith in absolute truth, the recourse to a methodical cruelty and the use of terror as a theological-political means of control. Betraying the insecurity of the *marrano* who wanted to assert his recently acquired Christian identity, Torquemada initially targeted the *conversos* and the Judaisers, and thus the Jews, guilty not so much for their alienness as for the fact that they did not allow the *conversos* to cancel their own foreignness and consign it to the past. This meant that Torquemada's ideal of purity was not founded on blood but rather on water and fire. A *marrano* could free himself from his own Jewishness and come to make up part of the New Spain. For the purposes of this purification, if the baptism water had not proven sufficient, then what would suffice would be the fire on the stake.

As Jacques Sémelin (2014) makes clear, over the centuries the intent to purify has been one of the factors for unleashing destruction. The purifying ideology in question may vary, but the sense of conviction is unchanging, hence the illustrious torturers' refusal to show any penitence. The protagonist of one sharp polemic that broke out in France was Paul Aussaresses, a general in the French Army, a commander of the Légion d'Honneur and a decorated veteran of the French Resistance. Having entered the French counter-intelligence service at the end of the Second World War, he practised torture first in the war in Indochina and then in the Algerian war. He was long considered a military hero and enjoyed an excellent reputation. That was, until he decided to break the silence and lay claim to torture as one 'weapon' among others. 'I do not regret it,' he declared in a famous interview. 'I did not like torture, but when I reached Algiers I resolved to do it. In that era, it was already in general use' (Beaugé 2000). He would return to this subject several times before his death in 2013, including in his memoir. And just as Torquemada became the symbol of the Inquisition, Aussaresses has become the symbol of French torture in Algeria.

Kaing Guek Eav, known as Duch, is among the very few individuals accused of crimes against humanity ever to have admitted the deeds imputed to them. He did so from his first court appearance in Phnom Penh on 17 February 2009. His life is linked to one of the darkest chapters in recent history, namely that of the Pol Pot dictatorship in Cambodia, which lasted from 1975 until 1979. Of Chinese origin but born in the Cambodian countryside, Kaing had a difficult childhood and youth, characterized by humiliation and discrimination. His release was his studies, in particular his study of mathematics, his engagement with French culture and, finally, communism. What proved decisive for him was his encounter with the charismatic Son Sen, his teacher, brother and friend, who would become one of the leaders of the Khmer Rouge. In 1967, Kaing entered the Communist Party and a few years later, taking the name 'Comrade Duch', he joined the Khmer Rouge guerrillas. The Central Committee charged him with organizing the M-13 camp in the Amleang forest. Among the prisoners here he met the young French anthropologist

François Bizot, at that time accused of being a CIA spy. In both the M-13 camp and in the M-99 camp which he had organized in Oral district, Duch honed his interrogation and torture techniques. When the Khmer Rouge entered Phnom Penh in triumph in April 1975, Duch was entrusted with the administration of the prison system and, most importantly, the infamous S-21 camp also known as Tuol Sleng, 'the hill of the poisonous trees'. The code 21 was allocated to the Santebal, the secret police that Duch directed.

In the camp, they were careful to keep the prisoners' deaths on hold, and instead subjected them to unspeakable torture. Sexual violence against women and girls was the norm. Bloody floggings and beatings were commonplace; electric shocks and red-hot metal tools were also used. The list goes on. All this and more is well documented, thanks to Duch's meticulous record-keeping. This ensured that even the photos of all the victims of the S-21 camp were conserved.

After the end of the Pol Pot dictatorship in January 1979, Duch abandoned the capital, though not without having first killed all the remaining prisoners personally. He vanished for a long period. Changing his identity and converting to Christianity over the ensuing years, he lived among the refugees in Cambodia and China. In 1999, an Irish journalist recognized Duch and interviewed him. Immediately after the interview, Duch handed himself in to the authorities.

There is some agreement among the various portraits that have been produced of Duch. For Rithy Panh, who directed the 2003 documentary film *S-21: The Khmer Rouge Killing Machine*, Duch has the 'mind of a mathematician', modest and courteous, with a mania for archiving and a fixation on order. The documentary sees the repeated use of a phrase formulated by Duch and which later gained wider usage: 'You can arrest someone by mistake; never release him by mistake.' A model teacher and an irreproachable revolutionary, he was convinced that he possessed the truth and that he was beset by the lies which he thought he detected everywhere. As he confessed to Bizot during one of their conversations, 'I find their [the prisoners'] duplicity intolerable. The only way is to terrorize them, isolate them, starve them! It is very hard! I have to force myself. You don't imagine how much their lies enrage me!' (Bizot 2006: 94). He was certain that a vast conspiracy had been prepared against the Khmer Rouge, and that his torture system had succeded in exposing it. He was an able organizer: he oversaw everything and noted down the confessions in detail, adding his own comments. And yet he admitted, 'I have never believed that confessions tell the truth.' His words are quoted in the account by Thierry Cruvellier, the French journalist who followed the trial, subsequently publishing the book *Le maître des aveux* (2011: 79).

Duch has been described in similar terms by psychiatric experts, particularly the psychoanalyst and Amnesty International member Françoise Sironi.[1] Duch's personal training took place in the cultural context of the time. As he put it, 'My only fault is that I did not serve God. I served men, I served communism': the need to fuse into the group; boundless commitment; the longing for recognition by the master or the superior; the need to serve; and the passion for obedience – all this, together with a deadly zeal and an extreme lack of human warmth, made Duch the prototype of the twentieth-century torturer, who dehumanized not only his victims but ultimately himself. In 2010 the UN-sponsored Cambodian tribunal sentenced Duch to life imprisonment for crimes against humanity.

Although he received the same sentence in Spain in 2005 – a total of 640 years in prison for crimes of 'torture, genocide and terrorism' – the story of Adolfo Scilingo, an officer of the Argentinian Navy during the Videla dictatorship from 1976 to 1983, was very different. 'I was at the ESMA [Escuela Superior de Mecánica de la Armada]. I want to speak to you.' That was how Scilingo contacted the journalist Horacio Verbitsky (2004: 15). This was the starting point of a long and disturbing interview published under the title *The Flight*. His revelations were like a thunderbolt, striking Argentina in every fibre of its being. On 2 March 1995, as soon as the book came out, the newspapers reproduced this officer's words and television stations broadcast parts of the taped dialogue. The effect was explosive. It was not the surviving

---

[1] See the transcriptions of the trial hearings: https://www.eccc.gov. kh/french/cabinet/caseInfo/61//E1_71.1_TR001_20090831_Final_ FR_Pub.pdf

victims or the victims' relatives who spoke but one of the butchers themselves. His account was all the more chilling because it came from someone who had denied every accusation for years, and it confirmed everything that had been surmised about the death flights. This time, the butcher's retelling corroborated that of the victims. And it allowed the re-emergence of a recent past that Argentina had in part tried to keep hidden.

Scilingo spoke of his work at the ESMA, the most famous of the dictatorship's internment camps, in the centre of Buenos Aires. Thousands were tortured there. In the so-called 'Dirty War', torture was the generals' preferred weapon. Most importantly, Scilingo clarified and detailed the preparation of the aircraft that set off from the ESMA towards Punta Indio, heading for the open sea. They went there so that the prisoners could be dumped into the ocean, so that they would disappear. They were *desaparecidos.* 'I find unacceptable the term *desaparecido*, and moreover the fact that I should have to bear it on my shoulders. I did not make anyone disappear, and nor did anyone else in the Navy. We eliminated an enemy in war' (Verbitsky 2004: 42). But something went wrong; Scilingo's defences crumbled. It happened during a flight in 1977. He found himself having to push one of his victims into the sea and suddenly saw himself in their shoes; he identified with them, recognizing the 'enemy' as a human being. The military machine, of which Scilingo had been a cog, broke down. He recalled this episode in the following terms:

> There are four things that make me feel bad: the two flights I did, the person I saw being tortured, and the memory of the noise of the chains and the shackles that were put on the prisoners . . . When I think about it I go out of my mind. Once they had lost their senses, they were undressed and when the commander gave the order, depending on where the plane was, the hatch was opened and they were thrown out, naked, one by one. That is the story. Macabre, but real – no one can deny it. I cannot make myself forget the image of the naked bodies laid out one after the other in the corridor of the plane, like in a film about Nazism. Skyvan planes from the Prefecture and Electras from the Navy were used. With the Skyvan, the bodies were dumped from the hatch at the back, which opened

from the floor. It is a very large hatch, but with no middle
position – it is either open or closed. So it remained open. The
NCO held down a sort of sliding door with his foot, in order
to leave a 40 cm space onto the void. Immediately after that,
they began to dump the subversives. In this situation, being
as nervous as I was, I almost fell, sucked toward the void.
(Verbitsky 2004: 54)

The glasses of whisky they downed, the sleeping pills they
swallowed to get through the night and the psychiatric drugs
they took to pull themselves together during the day did
nothing. Nor did he find any comfort in the words of the
military chaplain. Ensuring the Church hierarchy's *placet*, the
latter defined this as a 'Christian and not too violent' death,
and even referred to the parable calling for the separation of
the wheat and the tares. Scilingo found no peace: the void of
the sea devoured him. With each step he feared that he was
going to trip up. And the spectres of the unconscious faces
and the naked bodies persecuted him in his sleep.

'I am a murderer', he admitted in a TV interview. But these
devastating feelings of guilt, which he had not been able to
relieve, did not change his beliefs. 'It was something paramount that was being done for the country. A paramount act'
(Verbitsky 2004: 32). He called for some indulgence for those
who like himself had only followed orders. Yet even Thomas
of Aquinas, the patron saint of the Latin American Right,
contends in his *Summa Theologica* that, even though obedience is 'the greatest of all moral virtues', 'a subject may not
be bound to obey his superior in all things', if the latter commands something illegitimate (II, ii: 104, 5).

In short, it is high time that we recognized a crime of
obedience.

9   Born torturers?

Torturers display some common characteristics, but they are
also very diverse. So it would be a mistake to attempt to
generalize or draw up an archetype, a sort of amalgam of the
torturer. But this does not free us from contemplating a philosophical problem that is unavoidable in this context: namely,
the question of how torturers are made.

In order to understand the trauma of the victims, we have to enter the sites where the torturers are made. Studying the system of torture there, we have little difficulty in discovering – Sironi (1999) suggests – that 'one is not born a torturer but becomes one: either because of some violent deculturation experience, or through a specific initiation that uses the techniques of trauma'. Sironi advances this thesis on the basis of her psychoanalytic work. For example, she describes the training of the Greek political police during the colonels' dictatorship, when the torturers had to pass various phases of an actual initiation process. And she relates the case of a Bosnian teacher raped and tortured by young men who lived a few blocks away from her, who had until a few days previously been her students. How is it possible to transform into butchers from one day to the next?

Sironi's thesis is correct – but only in part. It is true that torturers are made rather than born. Yet not everyone becomes a torturer. Even under a totalitarian regime, personal responsibility is inescapable. Civil disobedience then becomes an obligation. This was the big question posed by Arendt during the Eichmann trial in 1963.

In 1950, Adorno had published his research on the authoritarian personality – the result of a rigid education and a discriminatory prejudice, which harboured a potential cryptofascism. This very controversial research contributed decisively to the replacement of the figure of the monstrous villain with that of the human criminal (see Montagut 2014: 57 ff.). Arendt, too, made the villain human, even while being cautious about the authoritarian personality.

The monstrosity of a villain's actions does not lie within him – in his supposedly monstrous nature – but rather in his inability to think about these actions and their effects. Eichmann was neither the beast from the abyss, nor a fallen angel; there was nothing demonic about him, nor anything profound or 'of the abyss'. Upon close inspection, he was a dull bureaucrat, a grey civil servant who remained faithful to his responsibilities in his post. Eichmann was not a monster – if anything, he was a buffoon.

The banality lay in the stupidity, the *Gedankenlosigkeit*, of the scandalous aloofness that prevented him from reflecting on his own actions, in the thoughtlessness that stopped him from placing himself in others' shoes. Neither monstrous nor demonic nor even sadistic, the villain appears all too human. 'The trouble with Eichmann was precisely that so many were like him, and that the many were neither perverted nor sadistic, that they were and still are, terribly and terrifyingly normal' (Arendt 2006: 276).

Primo Levi shares and in large part reaffirms the idea that the diligent executors of inhuman orders were not, except in a few cases, born persecutors: 'Monsters exist, but they are too few in number to be truly dangerous. More dangerous are the common men, the functionaries ready to believe and to act without asking questions' (Levi 1995: 228).

Yet humanizing the villain like this also creates numerous problems. First are those that closely concern the debatable – and already widely debated – concept of the 'banality of evil', as applied to the crime of extermination (see Di Cesare 2018: 194). Apart from the undervaluing of the role played by ideology, as well as the tendency to make the ordinary villain a cog in the machine, thus freeing him from responsibility, perhaps the greatest risk is that in asserting the banality of evil and the humanity of the criminal, we end up banalizing the crimes themselves. Arendt herself pointed to this risk. After reading a 1973 essay on Hitler by Joachim Fest, she replied to the historian by citing a comment from Bertolt Brecht: 'The great political criminals must be exposed, and exposed especially to laughter. They are not great political criminals, but people who permitted great political crimes, which is something entirely different' (Arendt 2013)

The slippery slope is a dangerous one. This is demonstrated by the drift towards the humanized portrayal of the torturer – even when we make the necessary distinction between an executioner like Eichmann and a persecutor. This portrayal of the torturer is over-represented, almost to the point of eclipsing the victim; he can be given such a human face that he assumes the air of a gentleman, even a hero. But there is more. If the torturer is not doing anything out of the ordinary – just being an ordinary man – then ordinary innocents could also prove to be bloodthirsty monsters. Indeed, sometimes we read that there is a torturer nested within each of us. We thus arrive at the paradox that runs through the thought of recent decades, in more or less explicit fashion, where the obvious question is no longer 'Would I speak or not under torture?' but rather 'Would I resist the temptation to torture, if they ordered me to do it?' As Lacoste has suggested (2010: 4–7), this leads us to assume that evil lies dormant within each of us, and that it could manifest itself in extraordinary and exceptional circumstances.Thus, not only do we make everyone a potential torturer, but we end up banalizing torture itself.

Doubtless, there are countless factors that could push people to become functionaries of the despicable. We do not have to refer to any kind of pathology in order to recognize that attachment to a higher decision or subordination to an imperious authority are bases for carrying out depraved and cruel orders. Famous experiments in social psychology – particularly the one conducted by Stanley Milgram, beginning at Yale in 1961 just three months after the Eichmann trial, and that by Philip Zombardo at Stanford in 1974 – have shown how easy it is to push 'good people' into blind obedience, even breaking their own ethical principles. In Milgram's experiment, 65 per cent of the volunteers – two-thirds of them – went as far as administering very violent electric shocks of more than 450 volts to someone posing as a 'student'; very few of the volunteers withdrew from the experiment or dissented.

But even before we observe what takes place in laboratory conditions, we need only look at history. Christopher Browning has reconstructed the paradigmatic history of the German police's 101 Battalion, a unit of around fifty reservists in Hamburg, for the most part workers, civil servants, traders, fathers – 'ordinary men' – who were too old to be enrolled in the army. We could not say that these were either fanatics or convinced anti-Semites. They were sent to Poland, without any training, to carry out a secret mission – and at the point of departure, it was still secret, even to them. Their mission was to exterminate the Jews living in scattered villages across Poland. At dawn on 13 July 1942, they entered Józefów and rounded up 1,800 Jews. They selected a few hundred to deport and then killed the remaining 1,500 in a single day, including men, women and children. And they did not stop there. In little more than a year, they assisted in the deportation of 38,000 Jews and exterminated some 45,000, shooting them at close range. Some of them went as far as posing for trophy photos. Only a small proportion of these 'ordinary men' refused to obey. Reflecting on the massacre, Browning asked why so few of them refused to kill (1992: ch. 18). He ascribes these acts of human wickedness – committed by recruits who were officially encouraged to direct all their sadistic potential against an 'enemy' – to the powerful authoritarian police system instigated by Nazism, which relied on discipline and commanded loyalty.

The mechanics of torture, in which it is necessary to programme, measure and regulate the doses of the suffering inflicted, can only in part be compared to execution, even face-to-face executions. The act of torture requires perseverance and postulates a deep determination, a full and unconditional resoluteness. The torturer does not commit a violent act out of instinct – something that could happen to many of us. Rather, he is an expert in violence. In this regard Zimbardo, invoking the recent history of Brazil, underlines the difference between professional torturers and the death squads who spread terror on the streets, empowered by their anonymous impunity: 'For a torturer, the work could never be just business. Torture always involves a personal relationship: it is essential for the torturer to understand what kind of torture to employ, what intensity of torture to use on a certain person at a certain time. Wrong kind or too little – no confession. Too much – the victim dies before confessing' (Zimbardo 2007: 289).

Whatever their differences, what emerges in common from the portraits of torturers is a convinced allegiance to an ideological project, the mission to purify and the commitment to destroy. Torture demands that the victim be completely dehumanized. For the torturer, the 'enemy' in his hands must not retain anything human. Rather, she must be separated from the rest of humanity, and therefore also from the torturer himself. Only through such separation can the tormentor anaesthetize himself and be able to apply increasingly well-honed techniques without impediment. But it is not a given that this procedure will, in fact, work. Even inside the torturer there remains some hidden spark of humanity. This explains why the first steps are so difficult, notwithstanding the indoctrination and initiation he has undergone, and why the tormentor, who is primarily struggling with himself, must abstract himself from the sense of belonging to a common humanity. It just takes a cry of pain, a gesture of distress or even, as in Scilingo's case, a false step by the torturer himself for this spark to re-emerge and allow the human bond to be re-established.

10   *Pedro and the Captain*

There is then drama for the torturer. Degrading the other may rebound on whoever is doing it. In denying the humanity of the victim, the torturer also reneges on his own. The villain is first and foremost his own victim. Dragged into the abyss of destruction, as he passes from one to another in search of the infinite victim, the torturer repeats himself, multiplying the crime. He is unable to stop. It thus becomes impossible for him to find a way out, an escape route.

In her 1958 book *Persona e democrazia*, the Spanish philosopher María Zambrano examined the workings of the crime that is made possible in totalitarian regimes by way of 'divinization' – the absolute exaltation of the leader. For the subaltern accomplice, this translates into the seductive appeal of himself becoming a semi-god. Zambrano considers the figure of the torturer in a case study of the accomplice's role. Driven by the anxiety to exist and attracted by the promise of living at all costs, this 'nobody' gives in to the point of disappearing. He sacrifices himself as he plunges into the abyss of non-being, drunk on the absurd promise that 'you will be like gods'. Zambrano recognizes a diabolical trait in this spiral of destruction. And she advances a thesis different and almost opposite to Arendt's: the desacralization of the villain has ended up making his crime something ordinary (2000: 83): 'One of the weaknesses of European man around the turn of the century was that he did not believe in the absurd, in horror, in gratuitous crime, in the diabolical.'

Perhaps no text better portrays the torturer's ruin than the 1979 play *Pedro and the Captain*, published by the Uruguayan writer Mario Benedetti. The four-part drama amounts to a series of scenes of torture, one following the other in a crescendo of violence and atrocities suffered by Pedro. He nonetheless resists, giving in neither to flattery nor threats, and stands up to the Captain. An intense, conflictual, even intimate dialogue opens up between the two. Initially seeking to persuade Pedro to confess, the Captain tells him, 'I can put myself in your shoes; you'd have to be an animal not to understand, and I assure you, I'm no animal . . . To be a savage you've got to have been born a savage, and I wasn't born like that. But somebody's got to do it; that's war' (2009: 22). The beatings and electric shocks do not defeat Pedro. Indeed, it is as if he is persecuting the Captain, telling him, 'if you've got parents and a wife and children, it must be pretty fucked up to go home at night' (p. 42). The dialogue resembles a psychoanalytic session. Pedro asks: 'Let's see, tell me how it came about. Childhood trauma? Deep conviction?' The Captain replies with a shrug of the shoulders: 'All right, I'm an anti-communist' (p. 72), continuing:

> It's a long, drawn out story. . . . No deep conviction . . . just sort of one small temptation after another – economic or ideological, it hardly matters. But always little by little. It's true I got the final push at the School of the Americas. With short and bearable tortures to my own body, they showed me where the most sensitive spots are. But before that they taught me how to torture cats and dogs . . . The first tortures are horrible. Nearly always, I threw up. But there comes a time toward morning when you quit vomiting, and then you're lost. Because four or five nights later you start to enjoy it. You're not going to believe me, Sir . . . (Benedetti 2009 [1979]: 73–4)

Dumped on the ground, Pedro is now dying. He does not give any names, not Gabriel, nor Rosario, nor Magdalena nor Fermín. And yet he speaks – not of himself but of the Captain, of the future that awaits him, and what his wife and children will say of him when they find out that he was a torturer. Then he devotes a thought to his partner – calling her Aurora, an invented name – and his son Andrés, reminding us that he is a father who could have saved his own life, but chose not to betray. The Captain is now left alone, without an interlocutor or a way out for himself:

Pedro, you are dead, and I am too. By different causes, to be sure. Mine is a death by entrapment, by ambush. I got caught in the ambush and there's no way out. I'm trapped. . . . But although I can't see any way out, there's something that can work sort of halfway for me. I already know that Inés and my children may come to hate me if the details of what I've done and what I'm doing ever come to light. But if I do all this and still get nothing in return – like the way it's been with you up till now – there's no possible way I can justify it. If you die without giving up a single piece of information, then I'm a total failure, a total disgrace. But if you do say something, that would give me some justification. It would mean my cruelty hasn't been for nothing, it'll have accomplished its purpose. That's all I ask of you. I'm pleading with you. Never mind four first names and last names, just give me one name. . . . I don't know if you understand me: I'm not asking you for information here to save the regime, just for a little piece of information to save me, or rather, to save some small part of myself. (Benedetti 2009: 98–9)

11 The victim's secret

Perhaps the most troubling thing about torture, or the most perturbing – in the sense well-rendered by the German word *unheimlich* – is the torturer's pretence to extract the victim's secret, the *Geheimnis*, and take ownership of it. In this sense, we could say that torture is a technique for opening up the victim: it tears into the body and pulls it apart in order to expose the secret that is hidden inside. It tries to open up the shell of human skin in order to reach the concealed site that the tortured person is supposedly guarding. The outside is broken apart in order to grasp at the inside. The goal is to turn the inside out, externalizing it. Even when more refined means are used, this metaphysics of extraction does not go away. Drugs are injected to make the victim give up his secret. A dualism of external and internal remains, together with the myth of the interiority in which the most reserved content is kept out of reach. In a world of transparency, the very possibility of such arcana is intolerable.

Interrogation should be seen in terms of a secret and its extraction. Contrary to what is generally believed, the interrogation is not a conversation, an exchange of questions and answers, but is itself an instrument of torture. This is precisely what we ought to reassert when faced with so-called 'coercive interrogation'. As Canetti observed in his *Crowds and Power*, the question used in a rising crescendo is a 'sort of dissection':

> All questioning is a forcible intrusion. When used as an instrument of power it is like a knife cutting into the flesh of the victim. The questioner knows what there is to find, but he wants to actually touch it and bring it to light. He sets to work on the internal organs with the sureness of a surgeon. But he is a special kind of surgeon, one who keeps his victim alive in order to find out more about him and, instead of anaesthetizing, deliberately stimulates pain in certain organs in order to find out what he wants to know about the rest of the body. (Canetti 1981: 284–5)

The interrogation continues incessantly, allowing no breathing space. Silence brings only further, more pressing and inexorable questions. The response raises suspicion, sparks distrust and makes everything start from the beginning again. The verbal oppression crosses over into physical aggression. Closed in by the questions, the tortured person has no way out. If he remains silent, he has already signed his own conviction. If he speaks, betraying himself even before he has betrayed those close to him, he permanently discredits himself as a traitor. His truth will not, in any case, be believed. The truth is not the truth. For the torturer still covets the secret. There will always be something that may not have been revealed – the secret of the secret, the arcane of the arcane – that remains to be uncovered. And the interrogation resumes inexorably. Himself covered by darkness and protected by secrecy, the torturer is prepared to do anything to force the victim finally to give up his secret. But the confession is not itself the objective. To admit as much would amount to justifying the instrumental violence of the interrogation. Rather, the objective is to extract the secret because only in that hidden place is it possible to sense what is at the other's core:

> In the immense solitude of the struggle that the tortured man engages with his torturer, it is not only confession that is at

stake. For to reveal the secret, to confess, would mean folding to the torturer's omnipotent violence and thus suffering the atrocious transparency of losing one's personhood. The secret, an intimate opacity, are the very foundations of identity. To lose them – meaning, one's thought becomes transparent – is a descent into madness. (Viñar and Viñar 1989: 165)

Even if the victim did want to confess the secret, give names, indicate hideaways and speak to the very point of leaving himself naked, he would still retain a bedrock of secrecy. If this were violated, he would end up losing his own self. The dimension of secrecy is vital. For the secret is the recess of otherness in the heart of the private. It is what allows the non-coincidence between the self and itself, disturbing it, moving it, driving it again and again to transcend itself. The fulcrum – or better, the deepest depth – of existence lies in the secret. And that is what the torturer wants to dominate.

12   Saying the word 'torture'

While torture claims that it compels the victim to speak, in fact it silences him. This is its paradox, or better, the ambiguity within which it can recur under cover of silence. It is not easy to lift this cover. Over the centuries, it has allowed a whole population of anonymous victims to fall into oblivion, and for their never-recorded history to be hidden at the margins of official history.

Saying 'torture' is an arduous task, owing to the political role of speech and the conflictual tension between language and power. Language's task is to articulate what power has disarticulated. And that means bringing the tortured body back onto our tongues, restoring it to the community and its history.

The torturer wants to see the pain but does not want to hear the victim's desperate complaints and his chilling cries. Nor does he want them to leak out and spread to the outside world. This body made flesh cannot have a voice, not even the inarticulate voice of the scream. Power subjugates and overwhelms the tongue; violence silences it. The tortured man no longer manages to articulate his spasms, his pain, his torment, his stress and affliction. The gap that exists between body and language becomes insurmountable. After the victim's language has lost its hold on meaning, and dropped its semantics, it is degraded. It is reduced to the inarticulate sounds that burst out from the suffering body; piercing cries, disconnected stuttering and wheezing. And with this last breath, everything must finish in silence.

In turn, the butcher's language is itself hollowed out, reduced to an instrument of violence, humiliation and order giving. The butcher does not want to speak to the victim, even during the interrogation. His words are only one more blow, one more flogging. Torture destroys language and therefore the humanity of the human being.

The answer comes from starting again from the wheeze, picking up on that suffocated stutter and rearticulating it. Precisely because the last scene of the torture is consummated in extreme violence that closes the victim's mouth, reduces all to silence and consigns him to oblivion, it is only in speech that we can find any redemption.

13   On pain and suffering

Violence, beatings, mutilation, burning, electric shocks, humiliation, all kinds of privation: torture is the systematic imposition of pain. Surviving torture is not like surviving an illness, an anonymous accident or some external adversity. The suffering is more acute, and more difficult to bear, because it is inflicted by other human beings. Not by chance – a wound can be an involuntary or accidental matter – but consciously so (see Le Breton 2010). That is why torture is a trauma that intimately tears at the victim, undermines her relationship with the world and leaves scars that, visible or otherwise, struggle indefinitely to heal.

Pain, in its countless aspects, is present in the existence of each person. It takes hold in a point of the body, torments it and weakens its integrity. It is a forced entry into the self – the irruption of a non-self, the insinuation of an intruder, the persistence of something alien. Because it is extraneous to our own selves, it divides and separates. The tangible experience of a negation, it is immediately lived as an 'against' that takes hold 'within'; it is the non-me that has penetrated into me. It everywhere appears, invades, subjugates whoever suffers it, attaching him to his own limits, to his own vulnerable finiteness. And in this suspension, it demands an either temporary or enduring grief for one's own self. As Montaigne suggests in his *Essays* (II: xxxvii), it familiarizes us with death. And fundamentally it is death's advance into the heart of existence.

That is why pain goes far beyond the point of the stricken body and hijacks the person's entire existence and history. For centuries, the metaphysical dualism between body and soul has driven a conception of a simply physical pain, closed up in the flesh. As if the pain could not spread from there and also strike the *psyché*, the soul, the mind. As if this latter could be wounded and scratched only by some other more ethereal and impalpable pain, something vaguer and more elusive. Some more or less tendentious definitions of torture even overlook psychological pain and want to ignore it. That is what we do when we distinguish 'no-touch torture' ('white' torture) from 'real torture'. But apart from the definition provided by Amnesty International (2016a: 65) in almost all the others – even in the Convention Against Torture – the dualism between body and soul is still at work. So we then speak of 'suffering' in order to indicate the more elusive pain that troubles the psyche.

But what is the connection between pain and suffering? And what can we say about this latter? Pain itself puts into doubt any dualism between body and soul, the physical and psychological spheres, for it allows an indissoluble connection to take place between the two things that western metaphysics has purported to separate. Pain is not closed off in some fragment of the body, nor consigned to a journey through the nervous system. It is not a mere somatic wound. It cannot be measured; it is not the mathematical projection of an organic phenomenon, which could be reduced to something objective and natural. On the contrary, pain is felt. And interpreted. There is no pain without the person who feels it. The sensation is also perception, the act that articulates pain, which is thus read in the interpretative context of the individual, characterized by the particular alchemy of her own story. The break into the body is already a semantic articulation. Body and the senses blend together. It is impossible to distinguish between the injury inflicted and the wound that resonates through that injury. Suffering is the resonance of pain. Toothache does not remain trapped within the tooth: it shakes and overwhelms whoever suffers it, distorting her relationship with the world. Suffering is the name for the spreading of pain, its work of digging that invades and pervades our existence. The more intense, piercing, aggravated the suffering, the more the pain betrays an act of violence, and the penalty relates to an unjustified punishment. A blow does not always and everywhere have the same significance. If the victim is wounded by an other and, what is more, deliberately – or rather, with methodical doggedness – within a supposedly penal logic, which the victim finds incomprehensible and excessive, then the suffering saturates the victim and remains permanent and indelible, even after the wound has healed. This is the suffering of torture, which is therefore the most intense form of suffering. Paul Ricoeur has written in this regard (1989: 9): 'The physical aspects of torture ought not mask its true nature, which is to say the destruction of the mind, the devastation of the personality, by way of the loss of the self; in short, the aim of a humiliation sometimes worse than death.' He later returned to speak of torture, a suffering so radical that the victim risks adopting the butcher's own vision. He did so in his short intervention *La souffrance n'est pas la douleur*:

> What goal, indeed, is the persecutor pursuing by means of torture? The doctors who treat the torture victims tell us that in making them suffer the butcher aims not so much at their death as at their humiliation, through the condemnation the victim is driven to make against his own self: these doctors also speak of the shame that, so to speak, sticks to the soul of the humiliated. (2013 [1994])

Nonetheless, the suffering thus described is still missing one further qualifier, which can help us grasp its whole unbearable drama. And this is the adjective Levinas adds: 'useless'. The excess is not only a matter of quantities: in its excess, this suffering escapes any synthesis and breaks apart any order. It is impossible to summarize. 'Useless suffering', suffering for another, is the negativity of evil, 'the not of evil,

a negativity extending as far as the realm of un-meaning'
(2006: 79). To suffer is pure endurance. But here endurance
is not the flipside of action. Suffering cannot be compared
with non-freedom. It is not a degradation which strikes the
human being by limiting his action. The passivity of useless
suffering is more passive than receptivity. For it is a defenceless exposure to violation; it is vulnerability. Here pain does
not take on colours of affectivity; it is pain in its purely
malign character. An evil without pardon.

In this sense, torture is not, as some say, only excess; it is
not an intensified violence. Rather, it is to exacerbate the
vulnerability of the other, exploiting their defenceless nudity.

14   Surviving one's own death

Surviving, from the late Latin *supravivĕre*, means living above
and beyond, remaining alive after a disaster, a calamity, with-
standing difficult conditions. Above all, it means living longer
than others, staying alive when one's family members, one's
friends, those belonging to one's own range of existence, have
passed away. It is the bitter experience described in his book
Surviving by Bruno Bettelheim (1979) after he escaped the
Nazi camps.

But torture has a particular peculiarity: namely, that
whoever has been subjected to it survives not the death of
others, but rather her own. For this reason, it is the most total
and most intimate violation. To directly face one's own death
provokes a 'devastation of the *conditio humana*' (Sofsky
1998: 66). Repeatedly experienced, the gloomy shadow of
this closeness to the furthest limit – as if we were almost
already in the world beyond – projects itself over the rest of
the survivor's life. The violence of torture interrupts the continuity of life. The thread of continuity is broken for ever.

The death of the other leaves both the void of that person's
own singular and irreplaceable world, which has escaped and
disappeared, and the task of bearing the other and their
world, of taking on this responsibility, of welcoming it into
one's own world – which must, however, necessarily be a
different world, precisely because of the death that has taken
place. This labour of grief, which cannot be taken for mere

internalization, was summarized in Paul Celan's verse *Die Welt ist fort, ich muss Dich tragen* ('The world is no more, I must carry you') (1986: 97).

Through grief, a painful but human task, torture forces the survivor to find the words to rationalize the pain of her own death, a pain which has penetrated into all parts of her body, as well as her despair that her world has come to an end, is lost, has disappeared and been destroyed by that violence. This is an irreparable loss, the fracture that nothing can ever heal, for it strikes at the deepest foundation of her existence. It is not simply a watershed separating a 'before' from an 'after'. This can happen to anyone – just as it sometimes happens that we have to seek a thread of continuity amidst the fragmentation that disaggregates and shakes up life.

But the survivor is not only different; she is an 'other' to her own self, to the point that she is no longer able to identify threads and connections that might mend this split and bind it together again. Torture has projected her into another world, an unknown, unimaginable world without any limit, in which all boundaries are obliterated; it is the anti-world of absolute violence. She has been kicked out of the world shared by others. Added to this is a further injustice: the difficulty of finding the path back. Disorientation reigns. Returning to the shared world is an almost impossible endeavour because her extreme experience – one which others have not been through – isolates, marginalizes and distances her. She continues to be separated, removed; despite every effort, she no longer belongs with the rest. She never returns.

This is the most sinister result of the violence. This violence thus continues to act; it can enjoy a posthumous existence. The survivor remains alive, but she lives outside of her own world in an existential abyss. Only with extreme difficulty can she emerge from this abyss and again make herself at home in the world. This exile takes on tragic dimensions. This is the survivor's ruin. Every attempt of hers to reach into the beyond ends up running aground. For as long as it is difficult to restore familiarity and trust, it is alienness that will mark her future relationship with the world and with others. No one will ever be able to make the tortured person forget the catastrophic forced entry that has violated the confines of her body and destroyed the shield with which she once protected herself.

The violence does not weaken or fade. Once it has penetrated the depths, it strongly anchors itself there (see Scarry 1985: 52 ff.). And it is unrelenting. It constantly surfaces anew, oppressing the days and flooding the nights. It puts on the butcher's overalls; it often even takes on his face. This is the perverse mechanism well known to those whose work involves treating the psyche. For Sándor Ferenczi, this amounted to identification with the tormentor himself (1932). The torturer thus becomes a persecutor twice over: first, because he has devastated his victim in the past and, second, because he continues to erode her from within in the present. Shame, dishonour and degradation mix together in relentless memory from which the victim cannot escape, remaining within the torturer's field of action and under his power. Acknowledging the suffering means recognizing the effects of that power.

The survivor plays host to a battle fought within herself between the butcher's destructive invasion and a therapeutic reconstruction that neutralizes his influx. But the torture victim's trauma in losing her secrecy can also be an obstacle to treatment (Sironi 1999: 119 ff.). More than a hypothetical repairing of the trauma, treatment should perhaps be the space in which the survivor recovers her link with the shared world, in particular rediscovering her profoundly wounded sense of belonging to humanity (Duterte 2007: 73).

It is the verbalization of the suffering that undoes the tormentor's power. Even if it makes the memory more acute again, only speech can free the survivor from the cell injected into her by torture, opening the way for escape to beyond.

3

The Administration of Torture

To this sly law of the tradition-transmission of a noble doctrine can be added an extreme procedure that has always proliferated along the borders of institutions of truth and which, far from diminishing, like an archaeological phenomenon of history, constantly develops, becoming more and more of a "regular administrative practice", or a political "routine": torture.

Michel de Certeau (1986: 40)

1 Giulio Regeni: the body of the tortured

At dawn on 3 February 2016, Ahmed Khaled and his bus full of passengers had just set off on their usual route along the desert road linking Cairo with Alexandria. Suddenly, a punctured front tyre forced Khaled to pull over on a lay-by between the tunnel that leads to Rimaya Square and the slight ramp curving to the right in the direction of the Pyramids. As he tried to change the tyre, some of the passengers who got off the bus noticed a corpse in the trench beside the motorway. It was the body of a young man. It was impossible to tell from his features whether he was a foreigner.

A few hours later, at 11 am, the Egyptian press spread the news that a body had been retrieved, belonging to a man of around 30 years of age. Only at 5 pm did the Italian ambassador learn that the body that had been recovered was that of Giulio Regeni, the researcher who had gone missing on 25 January, the anniversary of the 2011 Egyptian uprising. In the meantime, Regeni's body had been taken to the Zeinhom mortuary for autopsy. Cairo's chief prosecutor denied that he had been subjected to torture. The Egyptian regime tried to put investigators off the scent by passing off Regeni's death as a road accident or a mysterious crime. But the Italian ambassador told the BBC, 'I saw that there were cuts, bruises, burn marks and broken ribs. There is no doubt that he was badly beaten and tortured.'[1]

While the regime kept silent, this body spoke volumes. The torture had lasted for several days. His torturers had tried to keep him alive for some time in order to extract information from him. An anonymous report sent from a Yahoo account, whose testimony should be treated with caution, reconstructed what had supposedly happened between 25 January and 3 February. This account pointed the finger at the Egyptian security apparatus and the criminal police in Giza, the district from which Giulio disappeared.

The anonymous writer revealed at least three details that could only have been known to Regeni's torturers or those who witnessed his torments (see Bonini 2016). On this account, Giulio was taken to the Giza barracks, and when he refused to answer questions about his contacts among the leaders of Egyptian trade unions, he was beaten for the first time. Then between 26 and 27 January, he was apparently transferred to a National Security headquarters in Nasr City, where he was tortured for 48 hours, during which we may suppose that he was only partly conscious.

According to this account, Giulio was 'struck in the face', 'beaten on the soles of his feet', 'hung from a door', 'subjected to electric shocks on sensitive areas', 'denied water, food, and sleep' and 'left naked in a cell filled with water and electrified for a few seconds every thirty minutes'. As he did not give

---

[1] See the account published on 26 February 2016 by the Egyptian daily *Al-Masri al-Yum* and translated into Italian by Matteo Colombo on the 'Truth for Giulio' blog: https://veritapergiulio.it/giulio-regeni-alcuni-fatti-ebc05251ed1a .qa1j9uj80

in, it appears he was transferred to the headquarters of the military secret services, who were determined to demonstrate their inflexible ruthlessness. They allegedly threatened to subject him to waterboarding and to attack him with trained dogs. Then, we are told, the torturers attacked his body with a sort of bayonet, repeatedly cutting him.

This account was confirmed by the autopsy that was carried out in Italy. Giulio Regeni suffered wicked violence: broken teeth, swellings, burning, broken bones and fibulas reduced to mush. His body had been used as a 'slate for horror', on which the torturers had drawn various letters of the alphabet with a blade, as if they wanted to send a coded message. Death came from an unnatural twisting of the neck which caused a split in the spinal column. Whoever stood in front of him had brutally contorted his disfigured face. After its recovery, the corpse was 'placed in a refrigerated cell in the Kobri al Qubba military hospital', while awaiting a decision as to what to do with it. It was then dumped by the side of the motorway. During the autopsy in Egypt, they had cut off part of the ears in an attempt to remove any trace of electric shocks (Bonini 2016). Afterwards, his mother said, 'I only recognised him by the tip of his nose. . . . All the evil in the world poured down on him. But why?'

The Regeni case brought to light the systematically brutal repression that the Egyptian security apparatus carries out against opposition movements. Moreover, it revealed the autonomy and the impunity that the apparatus enjoys (see Declich 2016). Regeni was in fact in Egypt partly with the intention of reporting on all this; indeed, he was there as a result of his dedication to his research and of his political and civic engagement. His tragic story, with such a painful epilogue, deeply shocked public opinion, not only in Italy and Britain. Many repeated the words, 'Giulio is one of us.' This was an identification in two senses: Giulio is like us and we are like him. On the one hand, feelings were stirred into action by a corpse that demanded justice, and on the other there was anxiety about a cruel fate that could easily have been anyone's. The transition from citizen to *homo sacer* is shorter than we imagine. The body of the man was meant to have disappeared, together with all traces of torture. Instead, it was recovered. And this body disturbed, disconcerted and terrified for another unconfessed reason: the body bore the marks of torture. It brought torture to the surface again, from where it had been hidden. It reappeared in the community that had tried to immunize itself against torture by banishing it from view, relegating it to the margins and delegating it to an administrative power charged with mounting the 'mopping up' operation in a complicit and oblivious silence. So here we have the tortured man's body, alongside the body of the community: a relationship of extreme tension.

Torture pays for others, pays for us and discounts the price of the community's very existence, almost as if it were its condition of possibility. De Certeau reflects on this in an unpublished text on torture. His words are harsh: 'The few who return from the prisons and the camps bear a message, inaudible to those of us who are spared, that the social order from which we benefit supports itself through its relationship with crime.' A regime that lacks the necessary credibility can obtain a simulacrum of belief from the body of the tortured man. The persecutor does not limit himself to ensuring the function of the torture regime by writing the law on the body – a law which the condemned man must decipher from his wounds, as in Kafka's tale. No, he wants more: the confession which will serve as confirmation of his own power. Thus he engraves in flesh the order that doggedly pursues the legitimacy it lacks, a legitimacy which it can only obtain by extorting a credit note from pain. Behind the phantom of the social contract, we can make out the wounds, the cuts and the burn marks on the bodies. Power purports to draw a consensus on their skin. Torture proves itself a means of immunization for the community, a system of caesuras for rendering it homogenous. This is possible thanks to political surgery. Authorized to cut up bodies in order to reshape and protect the body of the community, this surgery eliminates the scum, gets rid of the waste and wipes away the filth, so that through police manipulation a compliant public opinion might be satisfied with this clean-up.

2   Benjamin; or, on an ignominious institution

All power is a temptation to excess, all force is a promise of brutality, all punishment is the threat of a torment, all interrogation the risk of torture. The boundaries become enfeebled, with a slippery contiguity between the different sides; there emerges the constitutive ambivalence of the 'forces of order' at the frontier between the exercise of policing and the exercise of politics.

We know the etymology of the word 'police', going back to *pólis* and *politeía* in ancient Greek. 'Politics' also comes from this same group of words. Schmitt drew attention to this connection in his 1932 essay *The Concept of the Political*: 'It must be remembered that both words, politics and police, are derived from the same Greek word, *polis*.' It fell to the modern state to establish security and order within its borders, and to banish conflict to the outside. It was no longer politics but simply the police – synonymous with order and security – that would now be employed for this purpose. Over time, the meaning of the term narrowed, well-being was set aside and the primary aim of security was prioritized. However, the sovereign, or the sovereign authorities, maintained their power unaltered over order and security. They held these powers but could also relinquish them. The German term *Polizeistaat*, 'police state', coined during the 1848 revolution, denounced the drift of a sovereignty that exceeded any formal and jurisdictional limit.

The ambivalence remained, ultimately residing – as Walter Benjamin indicated in his text *Zur Kritik der Gewalt* – in a 'law-preserving violence[,] a threatening violence' (2007: 285). This was not a matter of a 'deterrent', as the 'uninformed liberal theorists' have it, because that would require certainty. Rather, the threat from law is uncertain, just as its target can be uncertain. This is apparent in the field of punishment. As Benjamin notes in the case of the death penalty, whoever challenges it sees – even if without perhaps being able to well explain it – that she is not questioning a degree of punishment, or particular laws, but rather the law itself. For within the supreme violence that decides on life and death, there appears the origin of the law in all its terrorizing power (see Esposito 2002: 34 ff.).

What Benjamin says about the death penalty also applies to torture, even when we make all the necessary distinctions. Torture also appears in that field that not only sees judgement passed on *bloßes Leben* – mere life, exposed and naked, even if there is no death sentence – but moreover sees law pass over into violence, and violence into law, as the sovereign puts on the persecutor's mask. The contiguity between sovereign and torturer, which is manifest in the moment of torture, remains totally intact even afterwards. The persecutor does not just apply the law but employs force. He is the agent of a violence which is, nonetheless, the violence of the law. The recent mutation in this figure, transforming from the ruthless jailer into the gentleman torturer, the charismatic and loyal agent-hero, does not change the terms of the question. If anything, in certain ways it aggravates them.

In one of the most famous passages in his text, after Benjamin refers to the death penalty he focuses on the almost spectral union between violence and law, as present in the police. The police as an institution is bluntly characterized in terms of its 'ignominy' (2007: 286); it can simultaneously use the law but also regulate it and decide its broad confines. The German word that Benjamin uses is *schmachvoll*, which also means opprobrious, where *Schmach* indicates dishonour. This is because the police are situated in that sphere where any separation between the violence that lays down the law and the violence that maintains the law is cancelled out. It is the sphere beyond laws that the sovereign also moves in when he proclaims the state of exception. The police do not, as is generally believed, limit themselves to merely administering the law. On the contrary, they interpose themselves wherever the state is no longer able to guarantee itself in those countless cases of legal obscurity in which intervention in the citizen's life is justified by invoking 'security'. Police violence is formless, just as its spectral manifestation in the life of states is elusive and widespread. Benjamin adds a further observation that will no longer be surprising after our discussion of torture: police violence 'is less devastating where they represent, in absolute monarchy, the power of a ruler in which legislative and executive supremacy are united, than in democracies where their existence, elevated by no such relation, bears witness to the greatest conceivable degeneration of violence' (2007: 287). This spectral presence, which can run riot without impediment, which can render itself impalpable and sometimes even hide away, finding protection and shelter in the dungeons and the hidden arcana of the state,

sheds light on the phenomenon of torture within democracies. Indeed, not only does torture not go away but, as it
assumes different but no less cruel and heinous forms and
modalities, it passes into an illegal or sometimes legitimated
clandestinity, which evades control and descends into brutal
abuse and oppression.

After 9/11, the sovereign openly put on the cop's uniform,
as it criminalized an enemy who was now stigmatized as an
'unlawful combatant' – and therefore, among other things,
could legally be tortured. As Agamben has noted (2000: 107),
numerous risks derive from '[s]overeignty's gradual slide
toward the darkest areas of police law'. However, this is at
least of theoretical-political advantage, for 'The sovereigns
who willingly agreed to present themselves as cops or executioners, in fact, now show in the end their original proximity
to the criminal.'

3   The G8 in Genoa

It was 2001, not long before the attack on New York's Twin
Towers. The summit bringing together the world's eight most
industrialized countries – the Group of Eight (G8) – was
planned to take place in Genoa from 19 to 21 July. The city
was subdivided into different areas: a 'red zone' i.e. the city
centre, the location of the summit; the 'yellow' one, considered a control zone; and the 'white' one, not placed under
surveillance. Access to the port was forbidden and the airport
closed to traffic. Genoa was in a state of siege, and the prefect
had been authorized to deploy the armed forces. A defensive
line had been set up in the 'red' zone, able rapidly to repel
any attempt to cross the outer limits. But, most importantly,
a radio communications system had been prepared. Via this
system, all the forces of order could maintain sole and direct
contact with the police headquarters, from which they would
receive information. For security reasons, police command
wanted to avoid the orders being transmitted between officers
in the field. This proved to be an error, for many of the units
present had come from outside Genoa and did not know the
city. There had been no lack of indicators of tension even
before the G8 began. On the morning of 20 July, black bloc

groups repeatedly clashed with the forces of order at different points across the city. The Tute Bianche ('White Overalls') march, which consisted of various 'no global' (anti- and alter-globalization) organizations, social centres and the Left, slowly set off from the Stadio Carlini at around 1.30 pm. This had been agreed with police headquarters, although a question mark remained over the 'red zones', which the anti-globalization marchers had said they wanted to enter. The demonstration that challenged the summit, its agenda and the decisions in the air was bound to play out in a spirit of civil disobedience.

As the train of protestors advanced, columns of smoke could be seen rising from a neighbouring street. This lit the touch paper. A company of around two hundred *carabinieri* (military police), located close to the march, had been left isolated; its commander did not have a map of the city. He received the order from headquarters to move towards Piazza Giusti. The route he chose exposed his company to the risk of crossing the path of the march. A few minutes before 3 pm, the *carabinieri*, kitted out with shields, flameproof overalls, CS tear-gas canisters and new fibreglass and polycarbonate 'tonfa' truncheons, attacked the peaceful march and dispersed the demonstators. A battle then broke out in the side streets, where a few hours later a *carabiniere* aboard a Land Rover Defender opened fire and killed the young protestor Carlo Giuliani.

The *carabinieri* attack on the demonstration – consisting of eight charges in just a few minutes – had not been ordered by anyone. Officially, at least. The European Court of Human Rights defined the attack as 'unlawful and arbitrary'.

Certainly, the violence in that moment and immediately afterwards was devastating: there were brutal beatings, thousands of defenceless citizens were terrorized and there were hundreds of arrests. Many mysteries shroud those days; while attention was devoted to the clashes, epoch-defining decisions were being taken on the economic crisis and the public debt. These were decisions that left a deep mark on the years that followed but at that moment they passed by almost unnoticed. Massimo Lauria Franco Fracassi's investigative film *The Summit* raised many questions. The directors stated in an interview that 'what was at stake was not just Italian, but global';

indeed, for this very reason there were at least 700 US agents present in Genoa. What we should take from this is the fact that other countries' secret services had properly planned what happened, strangling the 'anti-globalization' movement.[2] The former magistrate Roberto Settembre, Court of Appeal judge in the trial concerning the events at the Bolzaneto barracks, reported these dramatic events in a book of his (2014: 255). He spoke of 'terrible suspicions', 'shadowy manoeuvres' and 'wild projects'. So, too, did Vincenzo Canterini – commander of the First Mobile Detachment of the Roman police, sentenced to five years' imprisonment – who pointed the finger at a mysterious special operations group, known as the GOS, whose presence in Genoa has remained rather ghostly; its intervention in Genoa has never given rise to any names, nor indeed any documents authorizing its deployment (2012).

The forces of order took their revenge at night in the assault on the Diaz School, which at the time played host to around ninety protestors and journalists from various countries. On Saturday, 21 July, late in the evening, hundreds of police officers surrounded the school building and burst into its corridors. They attacked the defenceless people inside with ferocious and unprovoked fury. There were cranial traumas, bleeding, contusions, broken limbs, fingers and ribs and bloodied faces.[3] The episode was documented by photos and partial recordings by foreign television stations; it was reconstructed in the 2012 film *Diaz – Don't Clean Up This Blood*, produced by Daniele Vicari.

However, we have no photos to attest to what happened later in the 'Nino Bixio' barracks in Bolzaneto, a heavily populated district of Genoa. The barracks had been fitted out as a temporary prison to deal with any arrestees. The first of these arrived in the afternoon of 20 July and the last of them was brought there on the Sunday; all of them remained in the

[2] See the interview at https://www.youtube.com/watch?v=xIehPfh9EO0

[3] [The Italian text refers to this using the idiosyncratically term 'Mexican butchery', probably dating to the Mexican Revolution and most famously used by Prime Minister Ferruccio Parri to refer disapprovingly to the public display of the bodies of Benito Mussolini and his accomplices at Piazzale Loreto on 29 April 1945.]

barracks until 23 July. We do not know the exact number detained: it is estimated that there must have been more than two hundred. Some of them came from the Diaz School, whereas others were picked up from the streets, the squares, the emergency rooms of the hospitals where they had gone to seek medical help, the campsites where they spent the night and along the motorways as they were heading away.

Terror and disbelief come one after the other in the victims' testimonies, collected in the trial proceedings. When they came out of the rapid response unit vans, the arrested were greeted with the cry 'Welcome to Auschwitz!'. Their arrival was marked by humiliating insults and unexpected blows. Plastic handcuffs stopped them from defending themselves. Many of them were forced to stay still, with their hands above their heads, on the square opposite. Some policemen pepper-sprayed the eyes of those unable to cover their faces. Fascist anthems and the Roman salute set the tone for their arrival. *Faccetta nera* (a Mussolini-era song celebrating the conquest of Ethiopia) was played over the speakers in the cells. The tormentors repeated the dark sing-song, '*Un due tre, viva Pinochet; quattro cinque sei, morte agli ebrei; sette otto nove, il negretto non commuove*' ('One, two, three, long live Pinochet; four, five, six, death to the Jews; seven, eight, nine, the little nigger does not move us'). The fascist subculture, deeply rooted in the security agencies, manifested itself in its most perversely aggressive forms. Paul, a 38-year-old Englishman, recalled what one official said: 'They asked us, "Who is your government?", and another policemen directed the same question at the people standing next to me. They told us what we had to answer and we all repeated, "The police are the government". Then the policeman said "Right answer", and went off' (Settembre 2014: 73).

The verbal attacks and use of the stress position – i.e. imposing a posture that first causes pain and then causes the muscles to give in – were combined with death threats, denial of food and sleep, beatings inflicted with truncheons and burning with various types of flame (see Zamperini and Menegatto 2014).

Women were intimidated. 'They said that they would rape us during the night,' remembers Arianna. Some women in the infirmary were forced to strip off and do push-ups in front of the doctors and officials. Norwik and Deniz, two young German men, were forced to run along the ground on all fours with handcuffs binding their wrists. Many were branded on the face. Although she had a broken left elbow, Cosima had to keep her arm aloft for almost half an hour. One police-man threw a gas canister into the cell where Gaia and Elise were being held. This induced retching among the inmates – some even vomited blood (see Settembre 2014: 121).

These torments have a name: torture. This word, ventured during the trial, was systematically rejected by the lawyers defending the 43 accused. To this end, they could make easy reference to the Italian penal code, which does not stipulate a crime of torture. A large number of these crimes would not have been prescribed had they been given the name that they deserved. Torture – the word that was made taboo, forbidden and denied – repeatedly re-emerged in every deposition and every witness statement.

Underlining the gravity of these acts and the suspension of the rule of law itself, the Court of Cassation's proceedings regarding Bolzaneto ended on 14 June 2013 with seven found guilty and fourteen acquitted. While many of the crimes fell under the statute of limitations, the years of the trial docu-mented the tortures perpetrated in that dark night for democ-racy. Amnesty International defined the G8 in Genoa as 'the most serious suspension of democratic rights in a Western country since the Second World War' (quoted in ANSA 2015). On 7 April 2015, the European Court of Human Rights condemned Italy for 'torture'. This raised the need – also in terms of managing public opinion – for an imprescriptible crime to be established.

4   'No touch' torture: on Stammheim prison

Over recent decades, the technology of torture has been refined. This has been its response to the urgent demands of an administrative power that seeks to leave no traces. As it spreads in clandestine form, torture has abandoned its bloody practices and devised new methods more consonant with modern ideals, taboos and prohibitions. It has distanced itself from its traditional violent setting and avoids bloodletting.

Blood is that metaphysical essence with which even the most hidden recesses of the body seem to be concealed. It was once the fluid in which the butcher signed terror's signature, making the invisible visible. Yet the overly sacred aura surrounding blood, its intangible aspect, its inviolability, ultimately made some methods seem too archaic and repugnant. A bloodless torture that does not contaminate itself with this fluid, a torture which is performed outside bloody settings and, indeed, seemingly avoids direct contact with the body instead appears innocent and unblemished. This bloodless torture must not leave stains or marks. This is a 'no touch' torture. Each citizen can feel secure, no longer horrified or terrorized. The spectacle of bloodletting is pushed back into the past. This 'clean' torture, more appropriately administered by a technician than by a butcher, is well prepared for institutional use, if possible under a euphemistic name such as 'coercion' or 'pressure'. But for all that, modernized torture is no more humane or less violent. On the contrary, this 'white' torture works on distress, plays on fear and takes advantage of each victim's weak points. While it does not leave scars on the body, it deeply wounds the victims' very existence. It often irreparably undermines their centre of gravity, sows turmoil in their relation with others and breaks apart their relationship with the world. It seeks to disorient, as it subverts the connections between experiences and representations, between motions and concepts, between memories and past life – even to the point of triggering states of psychosis.

'White' torture, which very quickly spread on both sides of the Iron Curtain, consists of various techniques from isolation to forced sleep deprivation; restriction of food and water; distortion of the victim's sense of space and time; the use of blindfolds and hoods, prolonged darkness or violently harsh lighting; arbitrary variations between extreme degrees of cold and heat; the subjecting of the victim to a soundproofed environment, or exposure to constant noise; the use of the stress position; the manipulation of fear, for instance by setting aggressive and unmuzzled dogs on the victim; the expectation of torture; and faked announcements of execution. Indeed, Dostoyevsky masterfully portrayed the distress that such a simulated execution can cause in his autobiographical novel

The House of the Dead (2004 [1862]). There are countless ways of making a human being suffer; 'no touch' torture can thus serve as a laboratory in cruelty and torment.

In his famous book *L'Aveu*, which Costa-Gravas later translated onto the big screen, Artur London – the Czechoslovakian Jewish communist arrested in 1951 after being accused of Trotskyism – recounted the tortures to which he was subjected by the Stalinist regime until his 1955 release. He evokes the climate of suspicion and the interminable interrogations but most importantly the sleep deprivation: 'I had known the worst Nazi concentration camps, Neue Bremme, and Mauthausen, but the insults, the threats, the blows, hunger and thirst were child's play when compared to systematic lack of sleep, this infernal torture which voids man of every thought and turns him into an animal dominated by his instinct for self-preservation' (London 1970: 106).

In testimonies collected by Amnesty International, some Iranian political prisoners have described the consequences of being blindfolded:

> The worst thing in Elvin is being held blindfold[ed] for days on end waiting for someone to tell you why you are there. Some people are left blindfold[ed] for days, weeks or months. One man has spent 27 months like this. None of the prisoners appear to know what he is being held for. After 27 months, he sits, largely in total silence nodding his head from one side to the other. Sometimes he just sits knocking his head on the wall. Obviously, they keep people blindfold[ed] to add to the fear. But when they suddenly whip off the folds to question you, you are almost blind, the light is painful and you feel dizzy. You can't concentrate on any single thought. (Amnesty International 1984: 19)

But 'white' torture was already being used in the 1970s in western countries against those accused of terrorism. An emblematic case was the United Kingdom, condemned by the European Court of Human Rights on 18 January 1978 on account of the violent methods that British police had used to extract information from members of the Irish Republican Army.

With disturbing continuity, German medicine and psychology – which were once extensively implicated in

Nazism – have contributed to the development of refined coercive interrogation and detention techniques. Konrad Lorenz, a renowned ethologist who himself had a considerable Nazi past, was awarded the Nobel prize in 1973, the same year in which his research into human sensory deprivation was tested by industrious psychologists and neurosurgeons in various German prisons. Before the Red Army Faction members Andreas Baader, Ulrike Meinhof and Gudrun Ensslin 'committed suicide', they were held in total sensory isolation – with intense, constant and uniform light, white walls and a perfectly soundproofed cell, so that they could not even hear the sounds that they themselves made – inside the walls of the Stammheim maximum security prison near Stuttgart. This is portrayed in Reinhard Hauff's film *Stammheim: The Baader-Meinhof Gang on Trial.*

5   *Desaparecidos*: when death is denied

Disappearance is not always counted in the list of torture techniques. But even very recent history shows that it must be considered a special, further, yet by no means marginal case of 'white' torture. This was recognized in the International Convention for the Protection of All Persons from Enforced Disappearance, which the UN adopted in 2006.[4]

If we want to understand the full depth and significance of this phenomenon, we should first of all ask why it is decided to make the victim disappear. The alternative would be their detention – even for a long time – or else execution. It is possible that the need to get rid of a corpse would occasionally and unexpectedly arise, especially if the body bore obvious traces of torture. But the question assumes a different aspect when forced disappearance becomes systematic practice. So why, then, 'disappear' the victim? What is the ultimate purpose and meaning of these victims' disappearance?

Our thoughts turn to the Argentinian *desaparecidos*, the death flights and the Madres de Plaza de Mayo. Flights made up part of a very far-reaching project called Operation

[4] http://www.ohchr.org/EN/HRBodies/CED/Pages/ConventionCED.aspx

Condor. This operation was aimed at eliminating political opponents across Latin America, from Chile to Bolivia and from Peru to Uruguay. It was organized by secret services from around the continent, led by the CIA. But the mass use of military planes to get rid of bodies was a particularly Argentinian affair.

The testimonies of both victims and executioners tell us that those who were kidnapped were tortured, and that if they were still alive after that they were administered heavy doses of pentothal. With hoods placed over their heads and chains around their feet, they were taken to the military airport and loaded onto aircraft. During the flight, none of them knew what was to happen to them. They thought they were being transferred. On board the plane, the doctor did the rounds to ensure that the sedative effect was still working, and the nurse injected additional pentothal. The prisoners' chains were removed, together with their clothing. After reaching the open sea, they were thrown out of the aircraft.

For the victims' relatives – starting with their mothers – there now began an infinite wait. Silence fell and doubt crept in. Exhausting research and risky investigations did not bring any results. It was almost as if the victims' social death had been decreed from the moment of their arrest or, rather, that their non-existence was now validated. The lack of a body, and thus the impossibility of burying the victim, had devastating effects. The victims were doomed to remain as ghosts for ever. Argentina itself – still home to these phantoms, and indeed responsible for them – itself became a haunted cemetery. Almost anywhere in the country could be the site of an unknown, obscure tomb.

In 1981, the Argentinian writer Julio Cortázar published the incipit of a story in the *Revista de Occidente*. Its finale, which went well beyond the author's artistic imagination, was based on this very real history:

[A] group of Argentines decide to found a city on a promising-looking plain. Most of them, however, are unaware that the land on which they begin to erect their houses is a cemetery, of which no visible sign remains. Only the leaders know this, and they say nothing, because the place is suited to their purpose, being a smooth plain, burnished by death and silence, and providing the best possible surface on which to trace out their plans. And so the buildings and streets are laid out, the life of the people is organized and prospers, and very soon the city attains a considerable size and height. Its lights, which can be seen from a long way off, are the proud symbol of those who built this new metropolis. Then symptoms begin to appear of a strange disquiet – suspicion, fear, and the feeling of being persecuted by strange forces which denounce the settlers and try to dislodge them. The most sensitive eventually realize that they are living on top of death, and that the dead are able to return in their own way, and enter the houses, dreams and happiness of the city's inhabitants. What seemed to be the fulfilment of an ideal of our times, a triumph of technology and of modern life, wrapped in the cotton wool of televisions, refrigerators, cinemas and an abundance of money and patriotic self-satisfaction, slowly awakens to the worst of nightmares, the cold and viscous presence of invisible rejection, and of a curse unexpressed in words, but which stains with its unspeakable horror everything which those men have built above a necropolis. (Cortázar 1981: 91)

The disappearance undermines the entire community. It prevents the labour of grief; it impedes and inhibits memory. The impossibility of formulating the past suspends the present and blocks off the future. One of the goals of enforced disappearance is to deny the community the customary and indispensable rites of loss.

The lack of evidence, even of a death certificate, obliges the surviving relatives to make an impossible decision, perhaps years after the fact; namely, to decide, at a given moment, that the disappeared person will never be coming back. It is almost as if it were up to their family members to kill them. That is why enforced disappearance drives those who are left crazy. Not by chance have the Madres de Plaza de Mayo been called the 'Madwomen of Plaza de Mayo' (see Padoan 2008). Over the years, they have marched tirelessly around the pyramids in front of the Casa Rosada asking when, where, how. The white headscarf, the *pañuelo*, made from the first strip of cloth in which newborn babies are swathed, was not just a sign of grief or a protest symbol. It was a way of laying claim to the life that this disappearance wants to cancel out as if it had never existed – as if the death itself had evaporated and dissolved during the course of flight. Perhaps this was the most extreme illustration of the elimination of the *desaparecidos*.

The Nazis were masters of this. The extermination camps were fields of ash. The annihilation had to culminate in ash so that every trace of the victims disappeared. Even before ash obliterated their future, it allowed the crime itself to be negated. The victims were not permitted a burial, so even dignity in death was denied. Ash is a tomb of nothingness. Not even the victims' remains were allowed to survive. It was as if these lives had never existed at all (see Di Cesare 2012).

The Nazi political project was built on the denial of the crime, even denying the victim's very existence. The solution found by the Nazis was also adopted in the post-war period, for which it provided a precedent. The extermination of more than 30,000 *desaparecidos* ought to be framed in this context, and doubtless also seen as one of historical continuity.

In Argentina, the strategy of denial was institutionalized. At a press conference for foreign media in May 1977, by which time over half of the victims had already been killed or kidnapped, Jorge Videla suggested five possible types of *desaparecidos*: those who had headed into clandestinity; traitors eliminated by the guerrillas themselves; those who had vanished or committed suicide in order to escape the guerrillas; those whose bodies had been left unrecognizable by armed confrontations; and – he finally admitted – those who had fallen victim to 'excesses' in the repression conducted by the armed forces.

As the regime came under pressure, it tried to empty the concentration camps and the detention sites, hurriedly making the 'subversives' disappear. It is worth underlining that many of these latter were picked up at their own homes, in the street or at their workplaces. The so-called 'Dirty War' was a war in which no battles were fought.

This time, a humanitarian body managed to tear through the cover of silence. Starting in October 1978, at the request of other countries who raised questions about the disappearance of 304 Italian, 164 Spanish, 40 German and 36 French citizens, the Inter-American Commission on Human Rights (IACHR) carried out inspections in the Argentinian prisons, staged hearings with the families of the disappeared, interviewed politicians and listened to the voices of journalists. The final report, issued in 1980, was a charge sheet against the military junta, which was accused, among other things, of having made systematic use of torture. Moreover, despite the military secrecy over the death flights, the first news on the fate of the *desaparecidos* began to filter through. It was known that a lot of the detainees had not even been registered; it was assumed that the bodies of the anonymous dead remained in limbo. But that was before the waters of the Río de la Plata began to bring back the handcuffed, mutilated, disfigured corpses. The macabre spectacle repeated itself, as the river continued to deliver these mysterious payloads. News of this was in large part spread by the ANCLA, the clandestine press agency founded by the journalist Rodolfo J. Walsh. On 24 March 1977, in an *Open Letter from a Writer to the Military Junta*,[5] which Gabriel García Marquez classed as a masterful piece of journalism, Walsh wrote:

Fifteen thousand disappeared people, ten thousand prisoners, four thousand casualties, and tens of thousands in exile: these are the raw numbers of this terror. Since ordinary jails were filled to the brim, you created virtual concentration camps in the main garrisons of the country, which judges, lawyers, journalists, and international observers are all forbidden to enter. The military secrecy of what goes on inside, which you cite as a requirement for the purposes of investigation, means that the majority of the arrests turn into kidnappings that in turn allow for torture without limits and execution without trial . . . In this way, you have done away with any time limit on torture. When the prisoner does not exist, there is no way he can appear before the judge within ten days, as provided for in a law that was respected even at the heights of repression during previous dictatorships. This lack of time limits has been accompanied by a lack of restrictions on methods: you have regressed to periods when pain was inflicted on the victims' joints and internal organs, only now you use surgical and pharmacological aids that the old executioners did not have at their disposal. The rack, the drill, flaying, and the saw

[5] Reproduced in full, in English and Spanish, at http://www.jus.gob.ar/media/2940455/carta_rw_ingles-espa_ol_web.pdf

of the medieval Inquisition have reappeared in the testimonies of victims, alongside prods and water boarding, the latest innovations in torture devices. By repeatedly succumbing to the argument that the end of killing guerrillas justifies all your means, you have arrived at a form of absolute, metaphysical torture that is unbounded by time: the original goal of obtaining information has been lost in the disturbed minds of those inflicting the torture. Instead, they have ceded to the impulse to pommel human substance to the point of breaking it and making it lose its dignity, already lost by the executioner, as well as by you yourselves.

Walsh mailed the letter that same day, but no editor from either an Argentinian or foreign newspaper published it. On 25 March, he fell into an ambush that had been prepared for him with the aid of information that a comrade of his had revealed under torture. He refused to be taken alive, shot at his attackers with a .22 pistol and was killed in the returning machine-gun salvo. He, too, joined the ranks of the *desaparecidos*. According to some prisoners' testimony, his corpse, riddled with bullets, was ultimately burned on the ESMA sports ground, like so many others.

We should not imagine that the practice of enforced disappearances stopped at the end of the twentieth century. The forms and modalities of this practice have changed. But disappearances are everywhere widespread. Amnesty reported over 27,000 disappearances in Mexico in 2015, in large part at the hands of the state. The case of 43 students from a college in Ayotzinapa, of whom there has been no trace since September 2014, has sparked outrage and uproar, including in other countries. A chilling series of femicides took place in Ciudad Juárez near the US border, pointing to endemic violence against women (see Amnesty International 2003a). Only scattered remains were retrieved in the desert surrounding the city.

6   The CIA's global Gulag

The torture of the last half-century bears the brand of the CIA. It would be hypocritical to present the abuses committed by US soldiers in Afghanistan, Guantánamo Bay

and Iraq as if they were a *unicum*, an error without precedent made by a few irresponsible individuals. This would
mean deliberately abstracting ourselves from the long tradition that had built up in the struggle against 'communist
subversion'.
When the Iron Curtain fell across Europe, the human mind
became one of the sites of the Cold War confrontation. At
stake was mind control. According to the historian Alfred
McCoy (2007), this all began with the scandal created by the
spectacle of public confessions at the first Moscow Trials.
Even figures considered courageous folded without putting
up resistance. It immediately became obvious that the most
effective techniques were not those that resorted to physical
violence, but rather those that targeted the psyche. From
1950 onwards, the CIA committed itself to the extremely
expensive MKUltra Project, a secret programme aimed at
conducting research into human consciousness and honing
extreme mind-control techniques, from hypnosis to halluci-
nogenic drugs (particularly LSD) and from electric shocks to
sensory deprivation. Doctors, researchers and scientists took
part in the project, and renowned hospitals, prestigious universities and, of course, the armed forces also contributed.
Given that the CIA was the lead intelligence agency, it succeeded in mobilizing enormous resources to the point of
involving US society as a whole. And it also made use of the
expertise acquired by Nazi doctors such as Kurt Plötner, who
had experimented with mescaline on Jewish prisoners at
Dachau. The spy war against the Soviet Union proceeded by
way of mind control.
This was a real turning point in the cruel science of pain.
Psychological torture became NATO's secret weapon in the
fight against communism, and cognitive psychology was the
obliging handmaid of state security. The new paradigm
brought together two methods: sensory disorientation and
self-inflicted pain. Honed across years of practice, these
allowed the refinement of a synergy whose product is existential chaos.
This became clear from the results obtained as a result of
these methods when they were employed against the victims
of torture perpetrated by Augusto Pinochet's regime. The
Chilean psychiatrist Otto Doerr-Zegers (1992) imputed

numerous – sometimes irreversible – symptoms, from anxiety to paranoia, to the new phenomenology of torture that had been adopted in the preceding years. He spoke of a psychological theatre in which the torturers were the actors in a staged drama. Performed on a set with its own special lighting, sound effects and plot twists, it culminated in the destruction of the victim.

After drugs had proved ineffective, the CIA-funded experiment conducted by the Canadian psychologist Donald O. Hebb at Montreal's McGill University had a decisive impact. This experiment showed the devastating effects produced by sensory deprivation. No less important was the discovery of self-inflicted pain – as experienced, for instance, in the stress position. Here the will to resist is weakened because the victim perceives himself as the cause of his own suffering.

The CIA assembled and codified the results of this research in the Kubark Counterintelligence Interrogation manual, later simply called the KUBARK manual (Kubark is the CIA's codename for its own headquarters). Written in 1963, it was for many years distributed in all the countries under the US sphere of influence.[6] Another textbook on interrogation techniques was the *Human Resource Exploitation Training Manual*, which the CIA provided to the Honduran authorities in 1983. A third resource was the set of instructions for treating prisoners, drawn up in 2003 by General Ricardo Sanchez, commander of the US forces in Iraq.

These manuals, especially the KUBARK, with which the CIA has trained whole generations of torturers, contributed decisively to the indiscriminate spread of torture through myriad channels in Asia, Africa and Latin America. In 1971 alone, more than a million agents were trained across 47 countries. This allowed the CIA to be directly involved in foreign policy, starting with the Phoenix programme, which began under Kennedy's presidency and was then trialled against the Viet Cong in 1967. These manuals had an enormous impact in Latin America. The extreme techniques used by the dictatorships on that continent came directly from

[6] The manual is now available online at http://nsarchive.gwu.edu/NSAEBB/NSAEBB122/CIA%20Kubark%201-60.pdf

the democratic United States. Torture remained the linch-pin of the strategy pursued by the CIA, also by way of its top-secret 'Project X' – the documents for which have been entirely destroyed by the Pentagon. It is worth underlining the systematic duplicity at work here: the US Army officially abstained from torture, in accordance with the precepts of the Geneva Convention and its own field manual, yet the CIA violated all prohibitions against torture by experimenting and spreading new torture methods. Even as the United States presented itself on the international stage as the champion of human rights, Amnesty International was following the CIA's trail in order to uncover and report the torture that was going on behind the scenes. The techniques are reproduced with undeniable continuity and the methods are honed as the CIA's global Gulag grows bigger and stronger; a domin-ion, this, which is the linchpin of torture and is constituted of ancient bonds, established alliances, shared prisons, but above all by way of the ties of secrecy and the shared language of violence.

The CIA could rely on all this in the wake of 9/11. If torture has become the privileged weapon of the 'war on terror', this is possible thanks to the CIA's global Gulag. The only difficulty is that while it had previously been able to recruit collaborators, this has become almost impossible in the struggle against jihadists – hence the intensification of heinous practices, the subcontracting of torture to third coun-tries and the involvement of large numbers of nations in extraordinary rendition (Committee Study of the CIA's Den-tention and Interrogation Program 2015). McCoy draws up the following balance sheet of the first two years of the 'war on terror':

[S]ome 14,000 Iraqi 'security detainees' subjected to harsh interrogation, often with torture; 1,100 'high-value' prisoners interrogated with systematic torture, at Guantánamo and Bagram; 150 extraordinary, extralegal renditions of terror suspects to nations notorious for brutality; 68 detainees dead under suspicious circumstances; some 36 top Al-Qaeda detainees held for years of sustained CIA torture; and 26 detainees murdered under questioning, at least four of them by the CIA. (McCoy 2007: 124–5)

7   Guantánamo: a camp for the new millennium

Orange, an otherwise radiant and happy colour, has in recent years become the symbol of torture. The photos of men in orange overalls, folded in on themselves and wasting away in steel chicken coops, have impressed themselves on the collective imagination. These men in orange are the terrorist subjects, the 'unlawful combatants', held by the US government at the Guantánamo camp in Cuba. Those who have demonstrated 'positive behaviour' – making up for their past guilt by collaborating – are instead dressed in white. These latter have left behind them the dense chain-link fence and the heavy green nylon tarps that separate Camp 4 – the wing for those with 'privileges' – from the metal cages of the infamous Camp X-ray, later renamed Camp Delta, the tomb of the men in orange. Guantánamo is the metonymy of the camp in the new millennium, the hyperbole of indefinite detention, the ultimate consequence of the state of exception, the back line and decisive front of the 'war on terror'. Yet 'Gitmo', as the army abbreviation has it, is the tip of the iceberg, the biggest and best-known camp in the CIA's global Gulag. We know little about other secret camps, like the one set up within the US airbase at Bagram in Afghanistan; we will perhaps never find out about the other ones at all.

Guantánamo started operating on 11 January 2002. Exactly four months had passed since the attack on the Twin Towers. The US torture debate had already produced its first results: it had become possible to speak openly about the 'lesser evil' to be used in an emergency. A large section of public opinion had been convinced that it was appropriate to use violence against one person in order to prevent violence against many. This was all the more true, given that the distinction between 'torture' and 'coercion' was making headway, and given that for many – including liberals – it seemed reasonable and not hypocritical, as the journalist Mark Bowden would later explain (2003), to use a bit of force to obtain information from a terrorist. Moreover, on 13 November 2001 Bush had decreed the fate of the 'unlawful combatants'. They were to be damned without being convicted, expelled and yet detained, and confined in steel so that they could be subjected to the dark arts of 'coercive interrogation'. All that remained was to identify some remote but reachable point on the map, outside jurisdiction but under control; a US base on foreign soil. They chose Guantánamo Bay.

The first twenty terrorism suspects were offloaded from 'Flight 01' arriving from Bagram on the night of 11 January 2002. Two days later 'Flight 02' brought another thirty. The list of arrivals – and the very rare departures – is published on the site of the Joint Task Force Guantánamo.[7] The peak was reached in 2003, when there were 680 detainees, of 42 nationalities speaking 19 languages. Subsequently numbers gradually fell. In 2011, there were 172 detainees. The much-obstructed plan to close the camp, ordered by the Obama administration in 2009, led to only a few repatriations and far more transfers. There still today remain around ninety detainees.

One prisoner, who was interned for several months, later recounted his flight to Guantánamo in an interview with Amnesty International. Muhammad Naim Farooq said:

> that he had not been told where he was being taken, or why, when he was transferred [from Afghanistan] to Cuba in mid-2002. He said, 'We didn't know where we were going. We were without hope because we were innocent. I was very sad because I could not see my children, family and friends. But what could we do? Yes, we got enough food – but what does this mean? My mother lost her eyesight while I was there.' Muhammad Naim Farooq recalled that the tightness of his handcuffs during the transfer injured his wrists, and that many of his co-detainees were crying 'because of pain' or because they were 'getting mad'. (Amnesty International 2003b: 17)

At Guantánamo, time was suspended by the 'indefinite detention', as highlighted by Judith Butler (2004: 50–100). Torture is inscribed in the conditions of everyday life. The cell is a modular cage of 1.8 m x 2.32 m, a steel parallelepiped open to the elements on all four sides and sealed on top by

[7] http://www.jtfgtmo.southcom.mil/xWEBSITE/

reinforced cement and metal sheeting; the bed is an iron grid which takes up a good part of the cage. The goal is maximum isolation, total exposure and no privacy, even for the most private of moments. The prisoners come out of their cages for 90 minutes a week. But they always and only come out after they have put on a leather belt, secured by rings attached to two metre-long chains that bind the wrists and ankles (see Bonini 2004: 21 ff.)

In this human zoo where everything is prohibited, depression wears down the prisoners, eating away at their bodies and digging away at their souls. A sizeable team of psychiatrists administers psychiatric drugs. The damned men in orange overalls are kept alive – whether they want to be or not – on account of the information that they might be able to provide. Some have tried to take their own lives by refusing to eat. Others have attempted to hang themselves. But the top of the cage is too low, and even if they could push their head through a suspended noose, they cannot succeed in killing themselves. Rather, they are left at the mercy of convulsions that leave indelible marks.

The 'coercive interrogation' of al-Qaeda suspects is carried out in windowless cement bunkers, where the electric lighting is never turned off. There is no torture, of course, but ten severe methods, including waterboarding, in the form prepared by the CIA. Prisoners are fastened to a tilted plank, with their feet in the air and their heads down, while their arms and legs are bound in place. The water pouring down their throat produces pain and the effect of drowning. The Guantánamo commanders are permitted the use during interrogation of: stress positions for up to eight hours; hoods and blindfolds; twenty-hour interrogations; isolation for up to thirty days; exposure to extreme cold or heat; disturbed sleep patterns; dogs; sensory deprivation monitored by doctors; and 'ego-reduction' techniques, including interrogation by female inquistors or even sexual abuse. The few accounts from the interrogations conducted in the hangar at Bagram airbase, near Kabul, are chilling indeed.

Divisional General Geoffrey D. Miller, commander at Guantánamo from November 2002 until April 2004, was tasked by Donald Rumsfeld with 'gitmo-izing' the Abu Ghraib prison in Iraq. Human Rights Watch has accused him of committing war crimes during the torture inflicted on detainees.

8   Abu Ghraib: the photographs of shame

On 28 April 2004, the CBC programme *60 Minutes II* broadcast digital photo images from the Abu Ghraib prison in Iraq. With their subject matter varying from sexual abuse to torture, the photos portrayed prison guards of both genders, apparently taking pleasure from their appalling acts. They enjoyed it even to the extent that they posed for the camera, fixing their abject trophy in everlasting memory.

One photo immortalized US soldiers smiling as they stand over a heap of naked and hooded prisoners. In another, a female soldier pulls a detainee's body on a lead. Photos show prisoners surrounded by ferocious German Shepherds ready to attack them. Others are pornographic images in which young prisoners are forced to masturbate in front of a female soldier holding a lit cigarette, giving a smug high-five. Of the many photos, two in particular aroused indignation around the world. The first was that taken by Corporal Graner, in which the special agent Sabrina Harman is photographed stooping over the tortured, ice-wrapped body of Manadel al-Jamadi. She is grinning at the camera, thumbs up in approval. The second photo, which soon became an icon, shows the simulation of psychological torture: a hooded prisoner stands on a large box with his arms outstretched and electric wires attached to his fingers. These wires, only partly visible under the hood, were false electrodes, designed only to elicit apprehension. The prisoner was made to believe that if he had buckled he would have been subjected to a potentially lethal electric shock. These, then, were the results of the glorious mission that the US administration had entrusted to the US Army, of bringing democracy to Iraq and liberating the country from the tyrant and torturer Saddam Hussein. While the army top brass immediately hurried to reassure the world that these 'abuses' were the work of 'a few bad apples', the Defense Secretary Donald Rumsfeld merely stated, 'I'm not going to address the "torture" word' (Hochschild 2004). In response to Rumsfeld, Susan Sontag insisted that 'torture' was precisely what these acts should be called.

In any case, the photos lifted the lid on this Pandora's box and brought to light countless other cases of abuse, torture and homicide perpetrated not only at Abu Ghraib – the prison west of Baghdad, a few kilometres from Fallujah – but across the whole military prison system in Iraq. A fact then emerged which had already been partly suspected; that the interrogations of the detainees were conducted by the civilian contractors of the Titan Coroporation, with the collaboration of translators; and that it was the FBI, the CIA and other secret services, operating in total anonymity, who were giving orders to the military police guards in these facilities and who controlled everything that was going on in Abu Ghraib. Moreover, it was confirmed that there were 'ghost' detainees present in the facility, considered important on account of the information that they might be able to provide. These 'ghost' detainees, whose numbers the CIA has never revealed, were not officially recorded. This meant that if they did not survive coercive interrogation, their bodies could be eliminated and no trace would be left of them. According to the testimony of US soldier Ivan 'Chip' Frederick, this was what happened to the Iraqi Manadel al-Jamadi, captured in Baghdad on 4 November 2003. Taken to Abu Ghraib, he was beaten and hung from a hook during the interrogation. He died of suffocation. Subsequently, in order to prevent his body decomposing, it was packed with ice – and he was thus nicknamed 'the Ice Man' – while a CIA agent inserted an IV tube into his arm and had him taken to hospital as if he were still alive. It was said that he had had a heart attack. We would have known nothing more of this if, before 'the Ice Man' could thaw, Corporal Graner had not taken the photos that soon ended up on the Web, spreading with all the ease and speed that digital communication allows. There is no lack of precedents of butchers taking photos as a kind of trophy, like those taken by the 'ordinary men' discussed by Browning. But what is striking in the images from Abu Ghraib, besides the exhibitionism, is the brazenness of the soldier Lynndie England, her cheerful conceit so dramatically contrasting with this site of atrocities and suffering. The 'smiling torturers' make even more intolerable the 'vile farce' of torture (Cavarero 2007: 142–54).

Mistreatment, rape, sadistic games and sexual violence were everyday life in Abu Ghraib. It was intimated to the prison guards that rules and norms could be broken. Above all, they were trained to treat prisoners like animals. Night-shift guard Ken Davis reported that 'We were also told they're nothing but dogs . . . You start looking at these people as less than human and you start doing things to them you would never dream of and that's where it got scary.'[8]

The International Committee of the Red Cross directly pointed the finger at the Department of Defence. In his richly documented book *Torture and Truth*, Mark Danner (2004) demonstrates the complicity of Defence Secretary Donald Rumsfeld. In an April 2005 report entitled *Getting Away With Torture?*, the NGO Human Rights Watch points the finger at President Bush and his aides for having used linguistic acrobatics to allow a *de facto* torture, endorsing it as an indispensable weapon in the 'war on terror'.

> it has become clear that torture and abuse have taken place not solely at Abu Ghraib but rather in dozens of US detention facilities worldwide, that in many cases the abuse resulted in death or severe trauma, and that a good number of the victims were civilians with no connection to al-Qaeda or terrorism. . . . Unless those who designed or authorized the illegal policies are held to account, all the protestations of 'disgust' at the Abu Ghraib photos by President George W. Bush and others will be meaningless. (Human Rights Watch 2005)

But very few have had to answer for the abuse and torture at Abu Ghraib. Its leading architects did, indeed, get away with it.

9   Women and sexual violence

Sexual violence goes hand in hand with torture; it is the inevitable 'bass line'[9] that sets its rhythm. From its most violent forms to the use of threats, insults and derision, it strikes at the victim's dignity and strengthens the butcher's

[8] *The Human Behavior Experiments*, Sundance Channel, 1 June 2006.

power. This lord of the flesh can satisfy his own impulses as he inflicts pain on a body that remains at his disposal. For the tortured person, breaking of taboos, exceeding boundaries and indeed nudity itself – and for her these are moral barriers and binds – can be irreversible traumas.

In general, torture of a sexual stamp has an explicit and marked meaning. It can often have a supposed 're-educative' purpose, as if the contortion of the victim's body is effectively 'straightening it out'. The most emblematic example is that of of homosexuality. In 2009, Human Rights Watch published a report on abuses against homosexuals in Iraq (Human Rights Watch 2009).

However, women are the priority targets of sexual violence, if not the only ones. Particularly targeted are those women with the greatest exposure who lead opposition movements, voluntary bodies and human rights associations. Their intellectual and political independence represents a challenge to authority, which must be punished. The torture of women almost always assumes the form of rape. This violence is usually preceded and followed by verbal abuse and insults, body searches, gross and painful acts and humiliating treatment. The term 'battering' can refer to the threat of these painful and easily hidden practices (Card 2010: 227). Rape allegations are often quickly shut down or entirely ignored. The woman is instead considered at fault for having contaminated her own purity so she is even denied her role as a victim.

In this regard, we need to draw two questions into sharper focus. Only over recent decades has the victim taken on historical weight. Previously written out of history, over time and after many struggles the victim's perspective has become a central concern. This has made the boundary between public and private space rather more porous. Where the victim does have a voice, she will generally call for a fight against the violence that she also suffers in private. A violence that was in the past belittled and considered a private matter is now made public and demands the extension of state control (see Wieviorka 2005: 89). Thus it is very difficult to distinguish between public and private violence. But there is no doubt that when a

[9] A pun in Italian: *basso* is 'bass' but also 'base' as in 'vulgar' or 'low'.

soldier or a policeman unleashes violence on a woman in their custody, this is an act of torture for which the state is responsible. The sexualization that has become ever wider and more intense over the last century has also contributed to removing any watershed between the public and private spheres. This obviously is relevant to torture against women, although these torments have not always been sexual in character.

The heretical, unsubmissive, insubordinate woman in revolt, so masterfully described by Michelet, is the witch, in her nocturnal shadow as in her spectral guise (1863). She is an invention. Witchcraft was an evanescent crime, something between sacrilege and magic, which demanded torture, the harshest punishment. For four centuries, starting in the late fourteenth century, witchhunts spread at a changing pace across modern Europe, shaking the continent. The unmarried, old, poor, widowed, strange or marginalized women accused of witchcraft were tortured according to the rules of the *Malleus Maleficarum*, the 'Hammer of Witches', published by two German Dominicans in 1487. Inferior, wicked, inclined to sin – according to the mistaken etymology which derived 'feminine' from '*fe + minus*', 'lesser faith' – the always unreliable woman had to be subjected to torture so that she would confess this otherwise unprovable and inexplicable sin. The witch's confession is thus the mother of all proofs.

So the legal system becomes ever more inquisitorial. Witchcraft demands torture and torture feeds witchcraft in an unbroken cycle (see Levack 2013: 15). But the use of a red-hot poker is enough to eliminate the *stigma diaboli*, and burning at the stake is enough to get rid of the witch. Neither rape nor sexual violence is needed. On the contrary, the witch's body arouses horror and repugnance.

Conversely, in an era of sexualization, rape becomes the means of exercising power over a woman's body, even rising to the rank of a weapon of war, an instrument of terror. That is not to say that this primordial violence was lacking in previous centuries. But the novelty of the last twenty years lies in the systematic nature of rape, which from the wars in Yugoslavia to the persecution of the Tutsis in Rwanda has become mass violence (see Flores 2015).

The phenomenon flourished during the course of the First World War, first on the Balkan front and then in the Armenian genocide. As defenceless civilians became more involved in the conflict, violence against women exploded. One of the darkest chapters of recent history is the mass rape committed by the Japanese Imperial Army during the occupation of Nanking in 1937; this wave of rape and brutality was the immediate result of an ancestral ethnic hatred. If the Second World War was marked by frequent episodes of mass rape, the numbers increased in post-war years. In Bosnia, the Serb militias waged war also by way of 'ethnic rape', with the intention of humiliating their enemies and corrupting them via their bastard children. Here, rape symbolized the 'manly' victory of a stronger and more able people over a weaker one, unable to defend its own women.

Between 1992 and 1993, rape camps first appeared, designed for 'ethnic cleansing'. These were very different from the concentration camps; the latter, faithful to the principle of fertility and nation-state, never thought of impregnating Jewish women. Bosnia marked a decisive break with Nazism. Many fail to grasp this rupture, though Agamben invites us to reflect upon it (2017: 152). In Bosnia, rape assumed the sense of a genetic conquest, assimilating the lives of others in one's own *éthnos*.

In its multiple forms, which defy any rigid definition – as Joanna Bourke has observed (2007: 7) – rape has become so widespread that even the UN's Blue Helmets have repeatedly tarnished themselves in this area (Human Rights Watch 2014).

10   In the hands of the stronger

In its multiple and often hidden forms, torture also emerges outside the scenarios of war. It lies in ambush in 'total institutions' – in the sense that Goffman (1961) uses the term – and bears on all those internment facilities where the defenceless are in the hands of the strong. These structures range from maximum security prisons to penal institutions, psychiatric wards, camps holding foreigners, hospitals, nursing homes, centres for the disabled, institutions for minors and orphanages.

Inevitably, questions must be asked about doctors' responsibility in this regard. However much of an aberration this may be, given that the main task of medicine ought to be therapeutic, it is sadly necessary to emphasize not only doctors' complicity in torture, but also their direct and active participation therein. This ranges from the very blackest cases, like the experiments on Jewish patients in the concentration camps – whose results German science took advantage of in the post-war period – and in less well-known examples that are easier to hide, such as the pharmacological torture employed against prisoners in penitentiaries. The 1975 Declaration of Tokyo, stipulating among other things that 'The physician shall not countenance, condone or participate in the practice of torture or other forms of cruel, inhuman or degrading procedures, whatever the offense of which the victim of such procedures is suspected, accused or guilty' has made little difference.

Roman Polanski's 1994 film *Death and the Maiden* takes place in an unspecified Latin American country. The plot is taken from the eponymous play by Ariel Dorfman, a writer born in Buenos Aires who lived in Santiago de Chile until the 1973 coup. His parents were Russian Jews, from Odessa. The peak of the drama is the clash between Paulina Salas, tortured under the dictatorship, and the doctor, Roberto Miranda. His voice allows her to recognize him as her torturer. Robert Miranda is forced to confess:

The real real truth, it was for humanitarian reasons. We're at war, I thought, they want to kill me and my family, they want to install a totalitarian dictatorship, but even so, they still have the right to some form of medical attention. It was slowly, almost without realizing how, that I became involved in more delicate operations, they let me sit on in sessions where my role was to determine if the prisoners could take that much torture, that much electric current. At first I told myself that it was a way of saving people's lives, and I did, because many times I told them – without it being true, simply to help the person who was being tortured – I ordered them to stop or the prisoner would die. But afterwards I began to – bit by bit, the virtue I was feeling turned into excitement – the mask of virtue fell off it and it, the excitement, it hid, it hid, it hid from me what I was doing, the swamp of what – By the time Paulina Salas was brought in it was already too late. Too late . . . too late. A kind of – brutalization took over my life, I began to really truly like what I was doing. It became

a game. My curiosity was partly morbid, partly scientific.
How much can this woman take? More than the other one?
(Dorfman 1994: 41)

But the abuse of power and the recourse to violence also
characterize what Franco Basaglia called 'crimes of peace',
that is to say, those legal crimes – an oxymoron which
expresses their fully contradictory character – carried out by
technicians with practical knowledge, primarily psychiatrists,
whose job it is to discipline deviancy, impose consent and
regulate public order (see Nightingale and Stover 1985). Scientific theories serve to justify these practices. And we need
to get rid of any misunderstanding in this regard: the technician can also be the intellectual in the role of the functionary
of consent, whether he is aware of it or not. Basaglia writes:

> There is some significance in noting that in the last two
> hundred years, torture was officially meant to have disap-
> peared, as something suiting the *raison d'état* of 'civilized'
> countries. The forms of control that prevailed by means of
> the proxies, clerks, functionaries, and producers of ideologies
> were evidently sufficient to ensure order. Only in those coun-
> tries where the false freedom of needs represented by indus-
> trial development remains unknown, and where they are not
> yet familiar with the advantages offered by the use of the
> human sciences and ideologies as a form of social control is
> torture illegally practised, with all the characteristics of a lack
> of 'civilization'.
> But at two hundred years' distance, the 'uneasiness in
> civilisation'[10] seems to be bringing a reappearance of torture
> more or less everywhere. And what might most surprise us,
> here, is that this is a precautionary torture, in which those
> being tortured and killed have nothing to confess if not their
> own refusal to be massacred, destroyed, killed. It is a torture
> carried out in order to obtain unconditional consent, passive
> acceptance, adaptation to an ever more rigid and restricted
> norm that responds ever less to the needs of those who have
> to submit to it. *Raison d'état* is prevailing over the last human-
> ism, and violence is no longer afraid to show itself for what
> it is. (Basaglia and Basaglia 2013 [1975]: 21–2)

[10] [i.e. a literal translation of the original German title of Freud's
Civilisation and its Discontents.]

Torture is inscribed in the state apparatus, which is all the more coercive wherever spontaneous consent is limited and fading away. Power then leverages all the institutions of repression and calls on the functionaries of consent, who are employed to guarantee the 'scientific' and 'legal' character of the crimes concerned. Basaglia denounces not only psychiatrists' perverse collaboration in the torture carried out in Latin America, but also the coercive mechanism at work in western democracies. Whether in the name of punishment or rehabilitation, support or treatment, the crimes of peace that are perpetrated against the weakest, the defenceless, follow a repetitive schema of instutionalized violence. And – as Basaglia sees clearly – it is but a short step from the ordinary crime of peace to torture.

The degree of violence can vary depending on the institution, the ability to conceal what is taking place and the margin of manoeuvre available to the repressive power. But the risk of transgression, the temptation to make recourse to illegitimate force, is strongest in the police, which has the monopoly on that same force.

Federico Aldrovandi, Stefano Cucchi, Giuseppe Uva, Michele Ferrulli, Riccardo Magherini, Davide Bifolco: these are just some of the names of victims whose stories have sparked uproar and alarmed public opinion in Italy. Here are misdeeds that would have been consigned to oblivion if it were not for mobilization by their families (in particular), and for the majority of which no one has been found guilty.

11   Torments and torture marked 'made in Italy'[11]

The violence that surfaced during the G8 in Genoa and the abuse that the forces of order have recently committed against defenceless citizens in police stations or even on the streets of Italian cities are not unprecedented and isolated episodes.

---

[11] [In Italy the English-language phrase 'made in Italy' is widely used both as an advertising gambit for authentically Italian goods, and often more ironically as a reference to the country's particular foibles.]

However paradoxical it may sound, the country of Beccaria and Verri can boast of a long tradition in the art of torture. If after his rise to power Benito Mussolini could avail himself of the OVRA (Organisation for Vigilance and the Repression of Anti-Fascism) even in the immediate post-war period, the political police and the intelligence services repeatedly extracted confessions by torturing the enemies of the state. It was Lelio Basso (1953) who denounced the still widespread practice of investigative torture.

In the 'Years of Lead', an already well tested but sporadically used mechanism was employed in an ever more intense and systematic way. The target was the militants involved in the 'armed struggle', understood in a very broad sense. Between the late 1960s and the early 1980s, there was a great build-up of torture reports gathered by Amnesty and referred to parliamentary scrutiny. It is a long list of torture victims – above all members of the Red Brigades – and even this is probably incomplete. The reaction from those who had political responsibilities of the time was to deny, or at most play down, the seriousness of what was taking place as they invoked the needs of *raison d'état*. The first significant parliamentary *interpellanze* date to 1982. These formal requests for information were signed by exponents of the Proletarian Unity Party, the Radical Party and leading independents, who pointed an accusing finger at the 'severe methods' authorized by interior minister Virginio Rognoni. They spoke openly of the 'torture' inflicted on members of the Red Brigades. The Sicilian writer Leonardo Sciascia, himself a Radical MP, robustly condemned a state that was ready to carry out torture behind the scenes:

> I do not believe that there is a country in the world which today includes torture among its own laws: but in fact there are few countries in which the police, sub-police and crypto-police do not practise torture. In countries with little sensibility for law – even when they proclaim themselves its forerunners and custodians – the fact that torture is no longer part of the law has conferred a boundless freedom to practice it in a concealed fashion. (Amnesty International 1985: viii)

What has recently emerged from the murky depths of Italian history is a confirmation of what we already knew, or at least suspected. But this knowledge now bears the signature of the protagonists in that torture, adding their seal to the narrative already provided by the victims. In his *Storia della colonna infame*, Alessandro Manzoni (2015 [1843]: 55–6) cites Francesco Casoni's treatise *De indiciis et tormentis tractatus duo*, published in Venice in 1557. The illustrious policeman Umberto Improta, at that time deputy commissioner and operational chief in the fight against the Red Brigades, must have taken his cue from this as he coined the menacing nickname for one of his subordinates: 'Professor De Tormentis'. Present everywhere that torture took place, but always strictly in the shadows and cloaked in dark secrecy, De Tormentis appears as a key figure in the testimonies and accounts from those years. He earned this nickname on account of the great suffering that he dispensed. He came with his special squads, two of which had names that rivalled their chief's own; one was the 'Ave Maria Five' and the other 'The Avengers in the Night'.

Although he may seem like a character from a preposterous film noir, De Tormentis did really exist. The journalist Nicola Rao met him. In his 2012 book *Colpo al cuore*, Rao reconstructed the final outcome of the clash between the state and the Red Brigades – that is, in its unofficial version. Until now, it has always been asserted that the state got the upper hand over the *brigatisti* without ever resorting to undemocratic methods and the unspeakable weapon of torture. But that is not the case. And the official history will have to be rewritten. The decisive revelations come courtesy of Salvatore Genova, known as 'Rino', a former police commissioner and chief of the NOCS (Central Security Operations Service). 'Exactly what the terrorists said happened, did happen: they were bound and blindfolded, as was even written on a service order, and then they were forced to drink heavy doses of salty water.' Genova talked about De Tormentis during the interview that he gave to the journalist Gianloreto Carbone during the popular RAI programme *Chi l'ha visto?* on 8 February 2012, albeit without naming him.[12]

---

[12] Interview available online: http://www.rai.it/dl/RaiTV/programmi/media/ContentItem-f9f29993-8740-479d-bccd-97d252a45f74.html

The *Corriere della Sera* did, however, choose to reveal his identity in an article published on 10 February 2012 (Bufi 2012). De Tormentis is Nicola Ciocia, former chief of the Interior Ministry's Central Office for General Investigations and Special Operations' anti-terrorism unit. After a successful career, he took his pension in 2004, with the rank of commissioner, retiring to private life at his house on Naples's Vomero Hill. A member of (the tiny far-Right group) Fiamma Nazionale, he said that he had 'always been a Mussolinian fascist. For legality'. He denied ever having practised torture. Nonetheless, he let slip a reference to Enrico Triaca, mentioning that certain methods did not work on him. Arrested in May 1978, Triaca was subjected to waterboarding. He reported the torture, and as recompense for this he was himself convicted of slander. This happened to all the real or presumed torturers who were tortured in this period. It was claimed that the claims of torture were just one further weapon being used by the Red Brigades. Moreover, journalists like Pier Vittorio Buffa and Luca Villoresi, who reported on torture giving a welter of detail, were themselves arrested for refusing to reveal their sources. They were only released when two police officers very publicly declared that it was they who had passed the journalists the information.

Italian history is rich in mysteries that still await resolution. But we can now say that in its fight against the Red Brigades, the state dealt its *colpo di cuore* (blow to the heart) at the time of the Dozier kidnapping, and that this was undeniably a case of torture. The US Brigadier-General James Lee Dozier, a NATO commander for southern Europe, was kidnapped by the Red Brigades in Verona on 17 December 1981. No ransom was demanded for Dozier, which immediately raised suspicions that he had been killed. The United States intervened by exerting heavy pressure on the Italian government. Dozier was inexplicably released soon afterwards in Padua on 28 January 1982.

By no means was Dozier's release spontaneous, as institutional sources would have us believe. The special anti-terrorist squads were ordered to take tough measures. They could rough up arrestees, as long as they left no marks. There must be no deaths or injuries. For this reason, the experts in harsh interrogation – De Tormentis and his associates

– were called on for assistance. On 23 January, Nazareno Mantovani was arrested. First, they 'disoriented' him, and then he was handed over to De Tormentis. A few days later, Ruggero Volinia and his partner Elisabetta Arcangeli were captured, taken to police headquarters and put in cells where each could hear the other through the wall separating them. Arcangeli was stripped naked and subjected to sexual torments. In turn, Volinia was brutally beaten, and then taken to a small house that was rented as needed. Here he was subjected to De Tormentis's usual treatments. Four men bound him to a table and used a funnel to pour large quantities of water and salt down his throat. He spoke, and said what apartment Dozier was being held in.

The blitz was a success. The torture had an immediate effect. Antonio Savasta also spoke. There followed hundreds of arrests. Inexperienced officers took a stab at being torturers. But they also made use of simulated execution, as in the case of Cesare Di Lenardo. It took place in one city after another, one haul after another, in an upsurge that led to the irreversible destruction of the Red Brigades.[13]

The torturers could rely on amnesty and amnesia. Thus the Italian state entrusted the defence of democracy to the tortures of De Tormentis, an industrious Mussolinian fascist. Adriano Sofri has written that 'It does not matter if they used the name torture; it is not used in the *raison d'état*, and moreover the Italian Republic steers clear of recognizing the existence of a crime of torture. That would be superfluous, they say. It was enough to make sure that our backs were covered' (Sofri 2012).

Organized impunity, sabotaging investigations, amnesty and amnesia, *omertà* and silence – all these serve torture; they make it easier for it to spread and allow it to perpetuate itself. Nothing will change so long as former torturers can still walk through the corridors of power with impunity, trading their own support for the wiping away of any responsibility. Here the state is but amnestying itself.

The danger of torture lurks wherever power is conferred by law, wherever a monopoly of violence is held. In the

---

[13] For an overview, see the *Insorgenze* website, https://insorgenze. net/category/torture/

twenty-first century, the potential torturer is the policeman. But investigating cases of torture is also the task of the police. Hence this institution, whose spectral character Benjamin invited us to reflect on, paradoxically finds itself on both sides of the dividing line. Here emerges the constitutive ambivalence of the 'forces of order'. They stand at the unstable boundary between the investigation *into* power and the conservation *of* power, and at the precarious frontier between pure police activity and pure political activity.

This frontier is buckling even further under the blows of terror. And as terror is made into a spectacle, the policeman who ventures to torture the terrorist may even be praised as a hero by the television-viewing public. If the condemnation of torture has not led to its disappearance, then in an age of terror it is indispensable that torture bear the stigma of criminality. Beccaria's Italy could find itself in a pre-modern condition; that is, the condition of not having even set up a legal barrier against this crime, in the very period that is marked by torture's post-modern return. This would bring very grave risks.

This is all the more the true, given that the lack of a crime of torture ends up encouraging and justifying what is already a deep-rooted double morality. In this double morality, while certain cases from time to time move us to pity, the rest of the time we tolerate the intolerable. Recognizing that torture is a crime would mean breaking through an almost ancestral aphasia that has prevented public discussion and often helped feed the evasive character of politics.

Epilogue

In the ancient Greek tradition, the epilogue is the final part of a speech that seeks to move the listeners. In modern times, it is the conclusion that summarizes, recapitulates and draws out all the consequences. But *epílogos*, from the verb *epiléghein*, has the sense 'to add' but also – through its meaning linked to *léghein* – 'to choose'. It thus calls for a space for reflection where we discern and evaluate. And rightly so. Finally, there is the preposition '*epì*', which can also function as an adverb. Among its many meanings, it also means 'on' or 'about', in the sense of speaking about a given subject.

The epilogue could then be, more than a conclusion, an appeal to the necessity of the *lógos*, almost an encomium for discourse and a hymn to speaking. For the closest, most effective accomplice of torture is silence. Right from the outset, in whatever dark place it is perpetrated, amidst veiled threats and suffocated groans, torture wraps itself in silence, enjoys the aid of secrecy and aspires to oblivion. Getting rid of the traces is part of the crime. When it is at its most perfected, the organized disappearance of the body itself becomes a weapon of terror.

Torture has a leading role in the history of human destruction. It is no longer ethically legitimate or politically acceptable to continue to read its history in terms of the march of progress. Violence is not the prerogative of Antiquity, and torment and cruel treatment are not the sole preserve of primitive peoples. The black phoenix has constantly risen from the ashes anew to pursue its long and multiform existence. Even refined cultures have not succeeded in warding it off. Anything but. There is no civilization, no nation, no political regime that has not easily adapted to torture, that has not found a place within itself for this practice, between violated rules and proclaimed exceptions. Democracy is not in itself resistant to torture, and in no way does it guarantee that it has come to an end. The name of Abu Ghraib – among others – points not just to a stain but to that place in space and time on which grounds western democracy will be called to the dock, answering before the court of history for what it has done to human dignity.

There is a close link between torture and the other great endeavours of destruction: genocide and extermination. Torture plays a decisive role in the economy of evil. It surreptitiously prepares us for wickedness and tacitly accustoms us to brutality. The destruction that torture perpetrates is not the annihilation carried out by extermination. But even when making the necessary distinction, there remains a strong bond of continuity. Torture is not a step towards genocide and does not nod in that direction. Yet it does show the same destructive intent. Torture is not an isolated crime: there is always some organization operating behind the scenes. Even if it takes place under a veil of secrecy, it is nonetheless a public violence; even if it is committed against a single individual, it is also an attack on the community. To wound the humanity of one is to wound the humanity of all.

Today, no one can say that they do not know. The McWorld of information forbids us from dodging our responsibilities. The alibis of 'I didn't know' and 'I wasn't aware of it' have long ago collapsed. If torture has not disappeared, we can at least recognize some progress in this regard: namely, in the vigilance exercised by public opinion and the action of international law. But this also demands the incrimination of governments, who must answer for what they have attempted to hide. This work of surveillance seems all the more difficult in that power has changed in dimension, expanding across a much larger area – not only by way of multiple network connections, but also thanks to immense systems of control, registration and record-keeping, and via that impalpable panopticon mechanism in which an unprecedented repressive potential is today being concentrated. Faced with this permanent risk, our vigilance has to be permanent and global. There may be limited political space for NGOs and humanitarian organizations, which carry out unparalleled and arduous work. But what will defeat torture is the barrier of disobedience and words that break the silence.

References

Adorno, Theodor W. (2004). *Negative Dialectics*. London: Routledge.

Agamben, Giorgio (2000). *Means without End: Notes on Politics*. Minneapolis: University of Minnesota Press.

Agamben, Giorgio (2005). *State of Exception*. Chicago: University of Chicago Press.

Agamben, Giorgio (2009). 'Note liminaire sur le concept de démocratie', in *Démocratie dans quel état?* Paris: La Fabrique, pp. 9–14.

Agamben, Giorgio (2017). *The Omnibus Homo Sacer*. Stanford: Stanford University Press.

Alexander, Matthew (2010) 'Torture's Loopholes', *New York Times*, 20 January, www.nytimes.com/2010/01/21/opinion/21alexander. html

Alleg, Henri (1958). *La question*. Paris: Les Editions du Minuit.

Alter, J. (2001). 'Time to Think about Torture', in *Newsweek*, 5 November, http://europe.newsweek.com/time-think-about-torture-149445?rm=eu

Améry, Jean (1971). *Unmeisterliche Wanderjahre*. Stuttgart: Klett.

Améry, Jean (1980). *At the Mind's Limits*. Bloomington: Indiana University Press.

Améry, Jean (1994). 'Wann darf Kunst auf "Kunst" verzichten? Zu dem Filmwerk "Das Geständnis"', in *Cinéma: Texte zum Film*. Stuttgart: Klett-Cotta, pp. 87–90.

Améry, Jean (2002). *Jenseits von Schuld und Sühne*. Stuttgart: Klett-Cotta.

Amnesty International (1984). *Torture in the Eighties*. London: Amnesty International.

Amnesty International (1985). *Tortura negli anni '80*. Pordenone: Studio Tesi.

Amnesty International (2000). *Take a Step to Stamp Out Torture*. London: Amnesty International.

Amnesty International (2003a). *Mexico: Intolerable Killings: 10 Years of Abductions and Murders of Women in Ciudad Juárez and Chihuahua: Summary Report and Appeals Cases*, 10 August, https://www.amnesty.org/en/documents/AMR41/027/2003/en/

Amnesty International (2003b). 'The Threat of a Bad Example', 18 August, Index number: AMR 51/114/2003, https://www.amnesty.org/en/documents/amr51/114/2003/en/

Amnesty International (2016a). *Combating Torture and Other Ill Treatment*. London: Amnesty International.

Amnesty International (2016b). *Report 2015–2016: The State of the World's Human Rights*. London: Amnesty International.

Andersch, Alfred (1977). 'Anzeige einer Rückkehr des Geistes als Person', in *Über Jean Amery*, Stuttgart: Klett-Cotta, pp. 19–38.

ANSA (2015). 'European Human Rights Court Condemns Italy for Diaz "Torture"', http://www.ansa.it/english/news/politics/2015/04/07/court-condemns-italy-for-diaz-torture_40d8e9f7-0c1e-4535-b522-a9f9c6d66737.html

Antelme, Robert (1947). *L'espèce humaine*. Paris: Gallimard.

Aquinas, Thomas (1948). *Summa Theologica*, vol. 2. New York: Benziger Brothers, p. 1645.

Arendt, Hannah (2002). 'Reflections on Violence', in Catherine Besteman (ed.), *Violence: A Reader*. New York: New York University Press.

Arendt, Hannah (2003). *Responsibility and Judgement*. New York: Random House.

Arendt, Hannah (2006). *Eichmann in Jerusalem: A Report on the Banality of Evil*. London: Penguin.

Arendt, Hannah (2013). *The Last Interview and Other Conversations*. New York: Melville House.

Augustine, Saint (1913). *The City of God*, Vol. 2, trans. Marcus Dods. Edinburgh: T. & T. Clark.

Aussaresses, Paul (2001). *Services spéciaux. Algérie 1955–1957*. Paris: Perrin.

Bahar, Alexander (2009). *Folter im 21. Jahrhundert. Auf dem Weg in ein neues Mittelalter?*, Munich: DTV.

Basaglia, Franco and Basaglia Ongaro, Franca (2013 [1975]). *Crimini di pace*. Milan: Baldini & Castoldi.

Basso, Lelio (1953). *La tortura oggi in Italia*. Novara: Civiltà.

Bataille, Georges (1986) *Erotism: Death and Sensuality*. San Francisco: City Lights.

Beaugé, Florence (2000). 'Les aveux du géneral Aussaresses', *Le Monde*, 23 November.

Beccaria, Cesare (2015 [1764]). *Dei delitti e delle pene*. Milan: Feltrinelli.

Benasayag, Miguel (1986). *Utopie et liberté. Les droits de l'homme: une idéologie?*, preface by Pierre Vidal-Naquet. Paris: Éditions La Découverte.

Benasayag, Miguel (2005 [1981]). *Malgrado tutto. Racconti a bassa voce da prigioni argentine*, preface by David Rousset, Naples: Filema.

Benedetti, Mario (2009 [1979]). *Pedro and the Captain*, trans. Adrianne Aron. Santa Barbara: Cadmus Editions.

Benjamin, Walter (1999). *Illuminations*. London: Pimlico.

Benjamin, Walter (2007). 'Critique of Violence', in *Reflections: Essays, Aphorisms, Autobiographical Writings*. New York: Schocken Books.

Bettelheim, Bruno (1979). *Surviving and Other Essays*. New York: Random House.

Binding, Rudolf G. (1933). *Antwort eines Deutschen an die Welt*. Frankfurt: Rütten & Loening.

Bizot, François (2006). *Le Portail: naissance d'un bourreau*. Mercuès: Talents Hauts.

Blanchot, Maurice (1949). *Lautréamont et Sade*. Paris: Éditions de Minuit.

Bonini, Carlo (2004). *Guantanamo. Usa, viaggio nella prigione del terrore*. Turin: Einaudi.

Bonini Carlo (2016). '"Ecco chi ha ucciso Giulio": l'accusa anonima ai vertici con tre dettagli segreti sul caso Regeni', *La Repubblica*, 6 April, http://www.repubblica.it/esteri/2016/04/06/news/_ecco_chi_ha_ucciso_giulio_l_accusa_anonima_ai_vertici_che_svela_tre_dettagli_segreti-136996781/

Bourke, Joanna (2007). *Rape: A History from 1860 to the Present Day*. London: Virago Press.

Bowden, Mark (2003). 'The Dark Art of Interrogation'. *The Atlantic* (October).

Brecher, Bob (2007). *Torture and the Ticking Bomb*. Oxford / Malden, MA: Blackwell Publishers.

Browning, Christopher (1992). *Ordinary Men: Reserve Police Battalion 101 and the Final Solution in Poland*. New York: Aaron Asher Books/HarperCollins Publishers.

Brugger, Winfried (2005). *Rettungsfolter im modernen Rechtsstaat. Eine Verortung*. Bochum: Kamp.

Bufi, Fulvio (2012). *Corriere della Sera*, 10 February.

Butler, Judith (2004). *Precarious Life: The Powers of Mourning and Violence*. New York/London: Verso.

Canetti, Elias (1981). *Crowds and Power*. London: Continuum.

Canterini, Vincenzo (2012). *Diaz. La verità sulla sanguinosa note nel racconto di uno dei responsabili dell'ordine pubblico al G8 di Genova*. Milan: Imprimatur.

Carbone, Mauro and Levin, David Michael (2003). *La carne e la voce. In dialogo tra estetica ed etica*. Milan: Mimesis.

Card, Claudia (2010). *Confronting Evils. Terrorism, Torture, Genocide*. Cambridge: Cambridge University Press.

Cavarero, Adriana (2007). *Orrorismo ovvero della violenza inerme*. Milan: Feltrinelli.

Celan, Paul (1986). 'Grosse, glühende Wölbung', *Atembende. Gesammelte Werker*, Band II. Frankfurt: Suhrkamp.

Committee Study of the Central Intelligence Agency's Detention and Interrogation Program (2015). *The Official Senate Report on CIA Torture*. New York: Skyhorse Publishing.

Cortázar, Julio (1981). 'Reality and Literature in Latin America', *Index on Censorship* 6(81): 89–91.

Cruvellier, Thierry (2011). *Le maître des aveux*. Paris: Gallimard.

Danner, Mark (2004). *Torture and Truth: America, Abu Ghraib, and the War on Terror*. New York: New York Review Books.

Danner, Mark (2009). 'US Torture: Voices from the Black Sites', in *New York Review of Books*, 9 April, http://www.nybooks.com/articles/2009/04/09/us-torture-voices-from-the-black-sites/

De Certeau, Michel (1986). 'The Institution of Rot', in *Heterologies: Discourse on the Other*. Minneapolis: University of Minnesota Press.

Declich, Lorenzo (2016). *Giulio Regeni. Le verità ignorate. La dittatura di al-Sisi e i rapporti tra Italia e Egitto*. Rome: Alegre.

Delarue, Jacques (2011). *Storia della Gestapo*. Bologna: Odoya.

Dershowitz, Alan (2001). 'Is There a Torturous Road to Justice?,' *Los Angeles Times*, 8 November, http://articles.latimes.com/2001/nov/08/local/me-1494

Dershowitz, Alan (2002). *Why Terrorism Works: Understanding the Threat, Responding to the Challenge*. New Haven: Yale University Press.

Dershowitz, Alan (2004). 'Tortured Reasoning', in S. Levinson (ed.), *Torture: A Collection*, pp. 257–80.

Di Cesare, Donatella (2012). *Se Auschwitz è nulla. Contro il negazionismo*. Genoa: Il melangolo.

Di Cesare, Donatella (2018). *Heidegger and the Jews: The Black Notebooks*. Cambridge: Polity Press.

Doerr-Zegers, Otto (1992). 'Torture: Late Sequelae and Phenomenology'. *Psychiatry: Interpersonal and Biological Processes* 55: 177–84.

Dorfman, Ariel (1994). *Death and the Maiden*, https://vanderbilt .edu/olli/class-materials/Death_and_the_Maiden_script .pdf

Dostoyevsky, Fyodor (1969 [1880]). *The Brothers Karamazov*. London: Heron.

Dostoyevsky, Fyodor (2004 [1862]). *The House of the Dead*. New York: Dover.

Duterte, Pierre (2007). *Terres inhumaines. Un médicin face à la torture*. Paris: Lattès.

Edmonds, David (2013). *Would You Kill the Fat Man? The Trolley Problem and What Your Answer Tells Us about Right and Wrong*. Princeton: Princeton University Press.

Esposito, Roberto (2002). *Immunitas. Protezione e negazione della vita*. Turin: Einaudi.

Esposito, Roberto (2008). *Bíos: Biopolitics and Philosophy*. Minneapolis: University of Minnesota Press.

Fanon, Frantz (2011). *The Wretched of the Earth*. New York: Grove Press.

Ferenczi, Sándor (1932). *Ohne Sympathie keine Heilung. Das klinische Tagebuch von 1932*. Munich: Fischer.

Fiorelli, Piero (1953–4). *La tortura giudiziaria nel diritto comune*, 2 vols. Naples: Giuffrè.

Flores, Marcello (2015). 'Lo stupro come violenza di guerra', in S. La Rocca (ed.), *Stupri di guerra e violenze di genere*. Rome: Ediesse, pp. 139–50.

Foucault, Michel (2003). *Society Must Be Defended: Lectures at the Collège de France, 1975–76*. New York: Picador.

Foucault, Michel (2013). *Mal fare, dir vero. Funzione della confessione nella giustizia. Corso di Lovania*. Turin: Einaudi.

Foucault, Michel (2014). *Discipline and Punish: The Birth of the Prison*, trans. Alan Sheridan. New York: Vintage.

Glaberson, W. and Williams, M. (2009). 'Officials Report Suicide of Guantánamo Detainee', *New York Times*, 3 June, http://www. nytimes.com/2009/06/03/us/politics/03gitmo.html

Goffman, Erving (1961). *Asylums: Essays on the Social Situation of Mental Patients and Other Inmates*. New York: Random House.

Golden, T. (2007). 'Guantánamo Detainees Stage Hunger Strike', *New York Times*, 9 April, http://www.nytimes.com/2007/04/09/ us/09hunger.html

Greenberg, Karen (ed.) (2006). *The Torture Debate in America*. New York/Cambridge: Cambridge University Press.

Grossman, Dave (2009). *On Killing: The Psychological Cost of Learning to Kill in War and Society.* New York: Back Bay Books.

Harrasser, Karin, Macho, Thomas and Burhardt, Wolf (2007). *Folter. Politik und Technik des Schmerzes.* Munich: Fink. Interview with Manfred Nowak, pp. 27–40.

Hochschild A. (2004). 'What's in a Word? Torture', *New York Times*, 23 May, http://www.nytimes.com/2004/05/23/opinion/what-s-in-a-word-torture.html

Human Rights Watch (2005). *Getting Away With Torture?* Human Rights Watch 17(1)G, https://www.hrw.org/reports/2005/us0405/us0405.pdf

Human Rights Watch (2009). *'They Want Us Exterminated'. Murder, Torture, Sexual Orientation and Gender in Iraq,* 17 August, https://www.hrw.org/report/2009/08/17/they-want-us-exterminated/murder-torture-sexual-orientation-and-gender-iraq

Human Rights Watch (2014). 'The Power These Men Have Over Us', 8 September, https://www.hrw.org/report/2014/09/08/power-these-men-have-over-us/sexual-exploitation-and-abuse-african-union-forces

Ignatieff, M. (2004) *The Lesser Evil: Political Ethics in an Age of Terror.* London: Penguin: pp. 138–43.

Kafka, Franz (1919). *In the Penal Colony,* trans. Ian Johnston. http://www.arts.uwaterloo.ca/~raha/793CA_web/PenalColony.pdf

Kahn, Paul W. (2008). *Sacred Violence: Torture, Terror, and Sovereignty.* Ann Arbor, MI: The University of Michigan Press.

Kantorowicz, Ernst H. (1997). *The King's Two Bodies: A Study in Mediaeval Political Theology.* Princeton NJ: Princeton University Press.

Klossowski, Pierre (1991). *Sade My Neighbour.* London: Quartet.

Kramer, Sven (2004). *Die Folter in der Literatur. Ihre Darstellung in der deutschsprachigen Erzählprosa von 1740 bis 'nach Auschwitz'.* Munich: Fink.

Kraus, Karl (2001). *Diicta and Contradicta.* Urbana: University of Illinois Press.

KUBARK (1963). *Counterintelligence Interrogation.* Langley, VA: Central Intelligence Agency. https://nsarchive2.gwu.edu/NSAEBB/NSAEBB122/

Lacoste, Charlotte (2010). *Séductions du bourreau. Négation des victimes.* Paris: Puf.

Lafaye, George (1916). 'Tormentum', in Charles Daremberg and Edmond Saglio (eds.), *Dictionnaire des antiquités grecques et romaines d'après les textes et les monuments,* vol. V. Paris: Hachette, pp. 362–3.

Le Breton, David (2010). *Expériences de la douleur. Entre destruction et renaissance*. Paris: Éditions Métalillé.

Levack, Brian P. (2013). *The Witch-Hunt in Early Modern Europe*, 3rd edn. London: Routledge.

Levi, Primo (1995). *The Reawakening*. New York: Simon & Schuster.

Levinas, Emmanuel (2006). *Entre Nous: Thinking-of-the-Other*. London: Continuum.

Levinson, Sanford (ed.) (2004). *Torture: A Collection*. Oxford/New York: Oxford University Press.

Lifton, Robert Jay (2000). *The Nazi Doctors: Medical Killing and the Psychology of Genocide*. New York: Basic Books.

London, Artur (1970). *On Trial*. London: Macdonald.

Luban, David (2014). *Torture, Power, and Law*. Cambridge: Cambridge University Press.

Luhmann, Niklas (1993). *Gibt es in unserer Gesellschaft noch unverzichtbare Normen?* Heidelberg: C. F. Müller.

Manzoni, Alessandro (2015 [1843]). *Storia della colonna infame*. Milan: Feltrinelli.

Margalit, Avishai (1998). *The Decent Society*. Harvard, MA: Harvard University Press.

Mayer, J. (2007) 'Whatever It Takes: The Politics of the Man Behind 24', *The New Yorker*, 19–26 February.

McCoy, Alfred W. (2007). *A Question of Torture*. New York: Henry Holt & Company.

Merleau-Ponty, Maurice (1968). *The Visible and the Invisible*. Evanston: Northwestern University Press.

Michelet, Jules (1863). *La Sorcière: The Witch of the Middle Ages*. London: Marshall Simpkin.

Montagut, Muriel (2014). *L'être et la torture*. Paris: Puf.

Montaigne, Michel de (1958). *Complete Essays*. Stanford: Stanford University Press.

Nagel, Thomas (1972). 'War and Massacre', *Philosophy & Public Affairs* 1(2) (Winter): 23–44.

Nietzsche, F. (1989). 'On Truth and Lying', in *Friedrich Nietzsche on Rhetoric and Language*. Oxford: Oxford University Press.

Nightingale, Elena and Stover, Eric (1985). *The Breaking of Bodies and Minds*. New York: Freeman.

Orwell, George (1949). *Nineteen Eighty-Four*. New York: Harcourt Brace.

Padoan, Daniela (2008). *Le pazze. Un incontro con le madri di Plaza de Mayo*. Milan: Bompiani.

Perret, Catherine (2013). *L'enseignement de la torture. Réflexions sur Jean Améry*. Paris: Éditions du Seuil.

Peters, Edward (1996). *Torture*. Philadelphia: University of Penn-sylvania Press.

Portelli, Serge (2011). *Pourquoi la torture?* Paris: Vrin.

Posner, Richard A. (2006). *Not a Suicide Pact: The Constitution in a Time of National Emergency*. Oxford: Oxford University Press.

Press, Eyal (2003). 'In Torture We Trust?', *The Nation Magazine*, 31 March, http://www.thirdworldtraveler.com/Torture/Torture_We_Trust.html

Rao, Nicola (2012). *Colpo al cuore. Dai pentiti ai «metodi speciali»: come lo Stato uccise le Br. Una storia mai raccontata*. Milan: Sperling & Kupfer.

Rawls, John (2001). *Justice as Fairness: A Restatement*. Cambridge, MA: The Belknap Press of Harvard University Press.

Reemtsma, Jan Philipp (2005). *Folter im Rechtsstaat?* Hamburg: Hamburger Edition.

Rejali, Darius (2007). *Torture and Democracy*. Princeton and Oxford: Princeton University Press.

Rejali, Darius (2011). 'Torture and Democracy: What Now?', in Shampa Biswas and Zahi Zalloua (eds), *Torture: Power, Democracy and the Human Body*. Seattle: University of Washington Press, pp. 25–44.

Remarque, Erich (2008). *All Quiet on the Western Front*. New York: Ballantine.

Ricoeur, Paul (1989). Preface to *Médecins tortionnaires, médecins résistants*. Paris: La Découverte.

Ricoeur, Paul (2013 [1994]). 'La souffrance n'est pas la douleur', in Claire Marin and Nathalie Zaccai-Reyners (eds), *Souffrance et douleur. Autour de Paul Ricoeur*. Paris: Puf.

Salomon, A. (2001). 'The Case against Torture', *Village Voice*, 28 November–4 December, http://www.villagevoice.com/news/the-case-against-torture-6396352

Sartre, Jean-Paul (1949). 'Dirty Hands', in *Three Plays*. New York: A. A. Knopf.

Sartre, Jean-Paul (1984). *Being and Nothingness*. New York: Washington Square Press.

Scarry, Elaine (1985). *The Body in Pain: The Making and Unmaking of the World*. Oxford: Oxford University Press.

Schmitt, Carl (2007). *The Concept of the Political*. Chicago: Chicago University Press.

Schmitt, Carl (2005). *Political Theology: Four Chapters on the Concept of Sovereignty*, trans. George Schwab. Chicago: University of Chicago Press.

Sebald, Winfried Georg (2013). *Austerlitz*. London: Hamish Hamilton.

Sémelin, Jacques (2014). *Purify and Destroy: The Political Uses of Massacre and Genocide*. London: Hurst and Company.

Settembre, Roberto (2014). *Gridavano e piangevano. La tortura in Italia: ciò che ci insegna Bolzaneto*. Turin: Einaudi.

Shue, Henri (2004). 'Torture', in S. Levinson (ed.), *Torture: A Collection*, Oxford/New York: Oxford University Press, pp. 47–60.

Sironi, Françoise (1999). *Bourreaux et victimes. Psychologie de la torture*. Paris: Odile Jacob.

Sofri, Adriano (2012). 'L'uso della tortura negli anni di piombo', *La Repubblica*, 16 February.

Sofsky, Wolfgang (1998). *Saggio sulla violenza*. Turin: Einaudi.

Sontag, S. (2004). 'Regarding the Torture of Others', *New York Times Magazine*, 23 May, http://www.nytimes.com/2004/05/23/magazine/regarding-the-torture-of-others.html

Steinhoff, Uwe (2008). 'Torture: The Case for Dirty Harry and against Alan Dershowitz', in D. Rodin (ed.), *War, Torture and Terrorism: Ethics and War in the 21st Century*. Oxford: Blackwell, pp. 97–114.

Steinhoff, Uwe (2013). *On the Ethics of Torture*. Albany: SUNY Press.

Sussman, David (2005). 'What's Wrong with Torture?', *Philosophy and Public Affairs* 33(1): 1–33.

Szymborska, Wisława (2002). *Miracle Fair: Selected Poems of Wislawa Szymborska*, trans. Joanna Trzeciak. New York: W. W. Norton.

Terestchenko, Michel (2008). *Du bon usage de la torture ou comment les démocraties justifient l'injustifiable*. Paris: La Découverte.

Tolstoy, Lev (2017). *War and Peace*. New York: Dover.

Tugendhat, Ernst (1995). *Vorlesungen über Ethik*. Frankfurt: Suhrkamp.

Verbitsky, Horacio (2004). *El vuelo*. Buenos Aires: Editorial Sudamericana.

Verri, Pietro (2006 [1776]). *Osservazioni sulla tortura*. Milan: Rizzoli.

Vidal-Naquet, Pierre (1959). *Face à la raison d'État. Un historien dans la guerre d'Algérie*. Paris: La Découverte.

Viñar, Marcelo and Viñar, Maren (1989). *Exil et torture*. Paris: Éditions Denöel.

Walzer, Michael (1973). 'Political Action: The Problem of Dirty Hands', *Philosophy and Public Affairs* 2: 160–80.

Weber, Elisabeth (2012). '"Torture Was the Essence of National Socialism": Reading Jean Améry Today', in Julie A. Carlson and Elisabeth Weber (eds), *Speaking About Torture*. New York: Fordham University Press, pp. 83–98.

Wieviorka, Michel (2005). *La violence*. Paris: Hachette.

Winik, J. (2001). 'Security Comes Before Liberty', *Wall Street Journal*, 23 October.

Wisnewski, Jeremy J. and Emerick, R. D. (2009). *The Ethics of Torture*. London: Continuum.

Wittgenstein, Ludwig (2013). *The Big Typescript*. Oxford: Blackwell.

Yovel, Yirmiyahu (2009). *The Other Within: The Marranos. Split Identity and Emerging Modernity*. Princeton: Princeton University Press.

Zambrano, María (2000). *Persona e democrazia. La storia sacrificale*. Milan: Bruno Mondadori.

Zamperini, Adriano and Menegatto, Marialuisa (2014). *Relations technique-scientifique: Les conséquences de la violence collective du sommet du G8 à Gênes, Requêtes Azzolina et autres/Italie n.28623/2011*. Strasbourg: Cour européenne des droits de l'homme.

Zimbardo, Philip (2007). *The Lucifer Effect: How Good People Turn Evil*. New York: Random House.

Žižek, Slavoj (2002). *Welcome to the Desert of the Real*. New York/ London: Verso.

Žižek, Slavoj (2006). 'The Depraved Heroes of 24 are the Himmlers of Hollywood', *The Guardian*, 10 January, https://www.theguardian.com/media/2006/jan/10/usnews.comment

Index